MW00952781

How to Reduce Your Condo or Homeowner Association Costs – Now and In The Future

During these tough economic times, condo and homeowner association Board of Director members are increasingly being given an unpopular choice – cut off my left hand (reduce services and amenities) or cut off my right hand (increase fees). The ideal solution is to do neither by eliminating unnecessary costs and waste. But, how exactly do you go about doing that? Here is a practical "how to" guide to identify areas of opportunity and to help you lead such a cost reduction effort.

TABLE OF CONTENTS

TABLE OF CONTENTS 2
Warning and Disclaimer 4
PREFACE 5
BACKGROUND 7
HOW TO USE THIS GUIDE 12
TOP 10 COST REDUCTION AREAS 14
1. Arrear payment collection (See Appendix G) 14
2. Management Company Services (See Appendix I) 14
3. Administration (See Appendix J) 15
4. Utilities (See Appendix L) 15
5. Insurance (See Appendix M) 16
6. Purchased materials & services (See Appendix O) 16
7. Litigation (See Appendix P) 17
8. Preventative maintenance (See Appendix Q) 17
9. Reserve funding (See Appendix R) 17
10. Taxes (See Appendix S) 18

ON-GOING COST CONTROL MECHANISMS 19
A) Financial Management (See Appendix T) 19
B) Financial Risk Management (See Appendix V) 19

NO-FRILLS IMPLEMENTATION APPROACH 21
1. INITIATE THE COST REDUCTION EFFORT 21
2. DEFINE THE PROBLEM 22
3. STATE THE GOAL 23
4. IDENTIFY THE TARGETED COST REDUCTION AREAS 23
5. DETERMINE WHO WILL DO THE WORK 24
6. SANCTION THE EFFORT AND MAKE ASSIGNMENTS 24
7. MAKE COST REDUCTION DECISIONS 24
8. IMPLEMENT THE DECISIONS 25

COMPREHENSIVE IMPLEMENTATION APPROACH 26
1. INITIATE THE PROJECT 28
    1.1. Sanction the Project Definition Development 29
    1.2. Identify A BoD Member To Champion The Effort 29
    1.3. Gain Leadership Commitment 30
2. DEVELOP THE PROJECT PLAN 32
    2.1. Define the Nature of the Project 33
    2.2. Define Who Will Be Involved With the Project 39
    2.3. Identify Project Timing 42
    2.4. Define the Implementation Process 43
    2.5. Receive BoD Approval to Proceed 46
3. KICK-OFF THE PROJECT 48
    3.1. Orient the Project Participants 49
    3.2. Give Assignments 49
    3.3. Provide Background Information and Reporting Templates 49
4. DEVELOP DECISION PACKAGES 50
    4.1. Define the Problem/Opportunity 50
    4.2. Identify Causes of the Problem/Pertinent Information 51
    4.3. Identify alternatives 51
    4.4. Select the best alternative(s) 52
    4.5. Plan the implementation 53
    4.6. Create Your Decision Package(s) 53
5. DECIDE UPON "QUICK-HITTERS" TO BE IMPLEMENTED 55
    5.1. Team Leader (s) Present "Quick-Hitter" Recommendations 55
    5.2. BoD Makes "Quick-Hitter" Decisions 56

6.   DECIDE UPON ON-GOING COST CONTROL MECHANISMS 57
    6.1.   Team Leader (s) Present "On-Going Cost Control Mechanisms" Recommendations 57
    6.2.   BoD Makes "On-Going Cost Control Mechanisms" Decisions 58
7.   COMMUNICATE THE PROJECT RESULTS 59
    7.1.   Develop A Communications Package 59
    7.2.   Communicate To Association Membership 61
8.   CLOSE OUT THE PROJECT 63
    8.1.   Measure Results and Thank Participants 63
    8.2.   Complete and Archive Final Project Records. 64

SUMMARY 66

Appendix A – Cost Reduction Project Plan 67
Appendix B – Decision Package 80
Appendix C – Tally Sheet 81
Appendix D – Team Leader Instruction Package 82
Appendix E – Top 10 Cost-Savings Return Areas of Opportunity 87
Appendix F – Standard Format for Displaying Cost-Savings Information 92
Appendix G – Arrears Payment Collection 93
Appendix H – Sample Fee & Assessment Collection Policy 107
Appendix I – Management Company Services 112
Appendix J – Administration 123
Appendix K – Sample Association Site Map 133
Appendix L – Utilities 135
Appendix M – Insurance 151
Appendix N – Sample Maintenance Responsibility Matrix 159
Appendix O – Purchased Services 164
Appendix P – Litigation & Legal Fees 179
Appendix Q – Preventative Maintenance 189
Appendix R – Reserve Fund 201
Appendix S – Property Taxes 207
Appendix T – Financial Management 214
Appendix U – Sample Cash Flow Report 222
Appendix V – Financial Risk Management 223

ABOUT THE AUTHOR 238

INDEX 239

Terms & Conditions of Use Agreement 240

Warning and Disclaimer

The information contained in this document is offered with the understanding that it does not contain legal, financial, or other professional advice. Individuals requiring such services should consult a competent professional. The author makes no representations about the suitability of the information contained in this book for any purpose. The material is provided "as is" without warranty of any kind. Although every effort has been made to endure that accuracy of the contents of this book, errors and omissions can occur. The author assumes no responsibility for any damages arising from the use of this book, or alleged to have resulted in connection with this book. This book is not completely comprehensive. Some readers may wish to consult additional sources of information for advice.

PREFACE

The financial management of every condo or homeowner association is ultimately the responsibility of its Board of Directors (BoD). It is up to them to act and react to a tougher economic environment brought on by rising operating costs, increases in foreclosures and payment delinquencies, rising taxes, aging capital assets, and a host of other things that eat away at their budget. Most respond by either raising fees or cutting services. Either of these very unpopular actions will almost always be met with strong resistance from its members. There is however, another alternative – reduce and control the association cost structure and eliminate waste.

This guide provides proactive Boards with the tools and techniques to help keep their fees down and enhance their properties' value without comprising quality of life. It draws upon learning's from the corporate business environment and applies it to the world of condo and home owner associations.

This guide is not meant to provide you with volumes of background information or intended to make you an expert in the area of condo or homeowner association cost reduction. It will however, provide you with a good working knowledge of the subject along with the following:

- A step-by-step guide on how to reduce your current cost structure now and to control on-going costs in the future.
- A clear and concise plan of action that is founded in best practices, proven results, and does so in a manner that most effectively uses your valuable time.
- Freedom to follow different degrees of cost reduction aggressiveness and to make any changes that may be needed to fit your unique situation

- A recommended "Top 10" list of most probable candidates for immediate/future cost reduction
- The means to control your association costs on a day-to-day basis through the use of sound financial business practices and management processes.
- Sample documents of all the necessary forms, templates, and instructions needed to implement a comprehensive cost reduction effort.

This guide is specifically targeted towards anyone who has financial management responsibility for a non-profit condo or a homeowner association including; BoD member, Treasurer, President, or Management Company Agent/Manager. It can be used by any size association. You will find that it contains no fluff or filler. No theoretical discussions, no business school jargons. Just a practical and useful method for reducing your association costs.

BACKGROUND

A condo or homeowner association is similar to other corporations -- it is governed by a Board of Directors elected by the members and a set of rules called by-laws. Board members have certain legal and ethical duties and responsibilities, which includes financial management and cost control. Depending upon the nature of the Board make-up, this financial responsibility can be handled with varying degrees of proficiency. Likewise, any effort to reduce costs can be approached with varying degrees of proficiency.

Since condo or homeowner associations are normally managed by non-paid volunteers who serve as the Board of Directors, it introduces a unique set of problems that will likely to surface when trying to manage finances. They include:

- Lack of Experience - Many association Board members are not professionals. They may not have formal training or practical experiences to properly lead and manage a company – and make no mistake about it, their association is a company. Typically, for-profit Board members who are paid, have to compete on the open market with other candidates to get the job. That usually provides for a stronger pool of qualified candidates. Board members for these companies are usually the most senior and qualified that are available. You would never select a Board member because s/he was the only candidate available who wanted the job or to use it as an entry level position.

  With non-profit associations, the candidate pool can be weak and lacking. Reasons for someone running for a Board position may include:

–   No one else will volunteer to do it.

–   I want to protect my personal interests.

–   I want to help and give back.

–   I have a personal agenda.

–   I want to be "In the Know".

–   I can achieve a sense of self-satisfaction.

–   I can build my resume.

–   I can form valuable relationships.

–   I want to acquire status or power.

Unfortunately, reasons such as these are not what is needed to efficiently run a company or to properly manage its finances.

Financial problems faced by condo or homeowner associations are not unique to them. The same problems exist in all companies. Some leaders handle these issues well and some don't. It is only reasonable to expect that an association with inexperienced leaders will face a very rocky road. This is a formula for a company destined to "trial and error" approaches and one that spends all of its time on fixing problems, rather than from preventing them from occurring in the first place. The use of a Management Company is no guarantee of success either, as many of them and under-qualified and under-experienced in "leading" a company or managing its finances. They can be good at routine back-office jobs (accounting, web sites, maintenance requests, etc.) and enforcers (CC&R compliance, fee collection, etc.), but they are not company Board leaders.

Because of these conditions, you could have a situation where an under-qualified volunteer Board is thrust into running a company. Many will not know what to do, why to do it, or when to do it. It is not surprising that they have problems with their "investors" –

namely, the owners. It is also not surprising that they lack experience in managing large budgets and systematically reducing the cost structure of their association.

- Complacency - Complacency is one of the dangers that any organization faces, particularly if it has been in existence for many years. Over time, it is not uncommon to see increased association costs with things like landscaping, management companies, insurance, maintenance, etc. The natural response to cover this "cost creep" is to increase association fees or in some cases, to reduce the level of service. This is usually the path of least resistance and the easiest way for a BoD to react to the situation. Management Companies can also fall into the same complacency trap of just doing their day-to-day jobs and reacting to increased costs with Board requests for increased fees or reduced services.

- Lack of Resources - Any concentrated cost reduction effort requires time and effort – two commodities that may be in short supply with a volunteer Board. They typically have other demands on their time and it is often easier to simply increase fees than to partake in the thankless task of managing such a cost reduction endeavor.

So, in light of these inherent problems, how should an inexperienced, volunteer BoD, or any BoD for that matter, react to a need to reduce/control their costs? They could just jump in and do the best job that they can. They could hire a qualified management consultant or Management Company to assist them in exploring new opportunities. They could try to recruit more qualified volunteer Board members who have a strong business and financial background. But, probably, one of the most important things they can do is to first arm themselves with knowledge on what is possible.

That is where this guide can come into play. It will add to that knowledge base and point a BoD in a direction that eliminates wasteful spending. It tries to mitigate the problems associated with a non-paid volunteer Boards, by providing a best practice and step-by-step guide on exactly what to do.

If you are reading this book, you are likely facing some type of financial problem in your association and you are looking for answers. You have taken a very important step simply by recognizing that a change may be required in how the finances of your association are managed. For some, this may be a "tweak" and for others, it may be a "major overhaul". Reactive Boards come to this realization when the financial pain becomes too great and it forces them to do something. Pro-active Boards come to this realization when they see troubles on the horizon and try to bring about a necessary change before it is absolutely required.

Once the need for change has been accepted, you can consider several cost reduction options, depending upon the size and complexity of the association, the severity of the problem, the amount of cost reduction being sought, state laws and regulations, and the business maturity level of its BoD or Management Company. But, exactly what options should you examine and how should it go about making meaningful cost reductions?

This guide can lead a BoD along this journey. It is organized around two complimentary categories of cost reduction opportunity.

- Immediate Cost Reduction. The first method is a one-time quick-acting and focused cost reduction effort aimed at cutting costs and eliminating waste NOW! It is highly re-active and meant to "stop the bleeding" by restricting the outflow of all unnecessary spending. It examines the high cost-saving return areas of opportunity for an association and then quickly implements a plan to reduce costs. Cost reduction may be targeted at specific costs (accounts) or it can be approached as an organization-wide effort that examines all costs.

- Control On-Going Costs.   The second method is focused on controlling **ON-GOING** costs, which is an integral part of reducing your overall association's costs in the long-term. You don't want all of your hard fought immediate cost reductions accomplishments go to waste in a year or two by having them replaced by others that creep into your spending plan.

The best way to get the maximum benefit for your association is to simultaneously implement both costs reduction efforts. You would first embark upon a cost reduction effort that is focused on immediate cost reductions and then you would install/tweak your cost control mechanisms to prevent cost waste from entering the picture in the future.

Besides telling you what costs you can reduce, this guide also tells you how go about it. The implementation section offers you a no-frills approach which is highly focused, takes a minimum amount of time and effort, and is very informal. It also offers a comprehensive approach that examines all of the association cost drivers and presents a detailed project plan of the steps that should be taken in the form of a project plan. Although this second approach presents the most opportunity for cost reduction, it is also the most structured and resource intensive. You can follow either approach to the letter or you can adjust accordingly, depending upon the nature of your condo or homeowner association and the number of resources you have at your disposal.

HOW TO USE THIS GUIDE

The beginning sections of this guide present the areas of cost reduction opportunity that will give you the biggest bang for your effort. As we proceed into the implementation section, some of the methods will be more complicated, requiring more skill and resources. Perhaps not everything here will be practical for your situation.

Your job is to select which areas of cost reduction might give you the highest return for your association and then to pursue them aggressively and tirelessly. The more areas you attack, the better your chances of success, as the effect will be cumulative.

Read through this entire book once. Get a feel for how it is organized, what it has to offer, and the resources that are being made available. Then, read it again, recognizing that you will have to make a couple of initial decisions on how comprehensive of a cost reduction effort that you want to pursue.

1) The first initial decision you will have to make is how many and what immediate cost reduction areas do you want to focus your efforts upon. This can range from one to ten or more. These may be your highest cost areas or areas that you know are problematic.

2) The second initial decision you will have to make is whether or not you have adequate on-going cost controls in place. If they are weak, you will want to strengthen them using the recommended techniques in this guide.

3) The third initial decision you will have to make is how comprehensive of an implementation approach do you want to take. This can range from a very simple and informal one to one that is very structured and disciplined

Once you have collected some initial thoughts on what you would like to do, you should reduce them to writing in the form of a rough proposal that you can discuss with others.

You will find that this guide contains many real life examples and samples of written material that can easily be customized to fit your unique situation. Because they are contained within this book and not in electronic form, you will have to re-create these documents from scratch. There is another alternative that you may want to consider. Located at www.condopresident.com under the "downloads" section are electronic versions of this material that can be purchased for a nominal cost.

Finally, a few words on how this guide is organized. Due to the nature of the subject matter, there is a wealth of information contained for each area of cost reduction opportunity. For ease of presentation and to help the flow of the book, most of the detailed information is contained in the Appendices. This is where you will find the real "meat" including pertinent background information, alternatives to be considered, and recommended actions to be taken.

TOP 10 COST REDUCTION AREAS

In order to gain the quickest cost reduction benefit with the least amount of effort you will want to first focus upon the "quick-hitters" -- the Top 10 cost-saving return areas of opportunity. This low-hanging fruit is highly visible, easily obtained, and provides immediate opportunities for cost reduction. Furthermore, it can generate interest, support, and momentum for more ambitious initiatives.

Listed in priority order (highest to lowest cost reduction opportunity) the following provides a description of each "quick-hitter" category. You are reminded that the descriptions below are in summary form. A detailed discussion of the topic can be found in the referenced Appendix where you will find important background information and recommended actions that may be taken. As you will see, much of the background research has been done for you. It will be up to you to absorb the information, apply it to your unique circumstances, and then decide what actions you will take.

1. Arrear payment collection (See Appendix G)

Even though this is technically not a cost category, it should be the first thing an association examines to help remedy its cost problem. It is quick, requires no substantive change in practices, and is always preferred to raising fees or reducing services. Essentially it is collecting the money that is due an association from members who have not paid their fees in a timely fashion. Since this represents a "loan" that is past due, a more aggressive collection approach should be taken to stem losses before the amounts become overwhelming. This can also send a signal that monthly charges are not something you can let slip.

2. Management Company Services (See Appendix I)

If and how you use a Management Company to help manage your association duties, will be an important area to examine for cost reduction opportunity. This category of expense can run upwards of 30% of an association's annual budget -- money that you may be able to spend more wisely. Depending on the nature and severity of your financial situation, you may be forced to take on more of those duties even though it may not be your first choice. Elimination of some or all of the services, rebidding/renegotiation of the Management Company contract, innovative use of private contractors or specialty service providers, holding Management Companies more accountable for cost reduction, and/or "partnering" to jointly attack cost reduction, are all within the realm of possibilities.

3. Administration (See Appendix J)

A condo or homeowner association's administrative activities generally involve storing, retrieving, and integrating information for dissemination to association members and the BoD. With recent advances in technologies such as email, web-based services, self-serve pulling of information, electronic requests, automated response systems, auto bill paying and money transfer, inexpensive association websites, document scanning, etc., it offers an excellent opportunity for an association to simultaneously reduce its cost and improve its service.

4. Utilities (See Appendix L)

Rising energy costs (natural gas, oil, electricity) or increased utility costs (water, sewage, waste removal) are prompting many condo or homeowner associations to analyze their usage and to take steps to reduce or eliminate waste. Depending on the solutions, the payback can be fast or intermediate, with costs ranging from being free to being a long-term investment. Knowing where to focus your attention and how to prioritize are essential to developing an effective, realistic utilities savings plan. Since this can be a major expense for an association, it is a prime area of opportunity for saving current costs and/or heading off future costs increases.

5. Insurance (See Appendix M)

Insurance cost can also be one of the biggest costs to a condo or homeowner association. Knowing the specifics of your insurance policy and also being familiar with the property that the policy covers, can save you money now and for many years to come. An important feature to understand is what the individual condo unit owner insurance covers and what the association policy covers in the event of damage. There are several ways in which an association can lower its insurance cost including; reduce the insurance liabilities, increase the deductable amount, adopt a policy that the responsible unit owner's insurance will pay the association's deductable, specify that owner's unit insurance will be the primary coverage in the event of duplicate coverage, or shop around for a lower price.

6. Purchased materials & services (See Appendix O)

From time to time you should carefully examine every single purchased service cost that you incur. This can include Management Company, landscaping, lawn cutting, irrigation, snow plowing, pool/spa maintenance, property maintenance, attorney, insurance, bookkeeping/accounting, TV/cable, utilities, common area housekeeping, pest control, locksmith, pond control, etc. This examination shouldn't just focus on renegotiating prices or getting more bids. Rather, it should explore every way possible to reduce the cost or, ideally, eliminate it altogether. You'll find that if you focus on just one item at a time, you'll often be able to come up with some really creative solutions.

7. Litigation (See Appendix P)

One area often available for pruning is your legal expense that can be kept under control with a few basic strategies. The highest component of any association's legal expenses is litigation and you want to minimize it at almost any cost. It is the area most likely to wreak havoc with the budget because it's so unpredictable and with the high costs for an experienced trial lawyer, litigation can quickly become a sink hole for association dollars. There are many cost-savings opportunities to minimize the use of an attorney for other more routing aspects of your association's business.

8. Preventative maintenance (See Appendix Q)

A streamlined, proactive approach to the maintenance of an association's physical assets will pay you both short-term and long-term dividends. Preventive maintenance is an essential component that should serve as the core activity to any maintenance plan.   According to a recent report by Jones Lang LaSalle (a global real estate services and money management firm), an organization/association that spends at the industry benchmark level for preventative maintenance will experience a 545% return over time. That is a huge return on investment that can not be ignored. Simply put, preventative maintenance is one of the most significant cost effective methods of maintaining current equipment or extending the life of other association assets

9. Reserve funding (See Appendix R)

Most reserve professionals will tell you that your reserve fund should be "off limits" as a way for an association find to find their way out a deep financial problem. But, future funds will do you no good if you can not survive. The original assumptions for building a reserve funding plan may or may not still apply. A responsible BoD experiencing a tough economic time must examine every area of cost reduction opportunity, including the reserve funding strategy. It may very well find that it can find a more optimum balance between meeting current and future needs.

10. Taxes (See Appendix S)

Certiorari, or the act of challenging property's annual real estate tax assessment, is among the least understood ways in which an association can keep it costs down. The basis of certiorari filing is the fact that the taxing unit often makes mistakes in property valuations. Left unchallenged, these mistakes can go on forever, resulting in the overpayment of real estate taxes for as long as the building stands

ON-GOING COST CONTROL MECHANISMS

Hopefully have made some significant "quick-hitter" cost reductions and gained some all important breathing room to now focus your attention on preventing unnecessary or inefficient spending from occurring again in the future. These on-going cost controls will help prevent "cost creep" and help eliminate waste at its source.

Listed below is summary of each "on-going cost control mechanism" category. Go to the referenced Appendix for a detailed discussion.

A) Financial Management (See Appendix T)

The Board of Directors is required each year to prepare a budget which estimates the revenues and expenses for administration and operation of the condo or homeowner association. A budget provides a roadmap for the financial management of the association including controlling costs. Historical results along with the effects of current revenue and cost trends provide the basis for a budget and can help predict the future financial health of the association. A budget can also serve as a control tool for a BoD to carefully scrutinize unnecessary expenses or cost increases. The BoD can use its budget item approval/veto power to put strict controls on every aspect of association spending.

B) Financial Risk Management (See Appendix V)

General risk management policy identifies areas of risk, estimates the degree of risk, implements procedures and practices to reduce potential losses, and evaluates which losses to retain and which losses to cover with insurance. Financial exposures for a condo or homeowner association include theft of cash, fraud, embezzlement, loss of key records and business interruption, property and casualty risks, worker's compensation risk, and other liability risk in various forms. In order to eliminate or minimize a potentially damaging financial event, a BoD should consider implementing a variety of risk prevention measures to protect the association from financial loss.

NO-FRILLS IMPLEMENTATION APPROACH

The prior two chapters have given you some suggestions on **WHAT** you can do to reduce your association costs. Now, it is time to discuss **HOW** you go about identifying which ones you will pursue and **HOW** you will implement the changes. Two alternatives will be offered. In this chapter, the No-Frills Approach is discussed.

The advantage of this No-Frills Approach is that it can be quite informal and does not require a lot of structure or coordination. Also, it can be executed with a minimal amount of resources (time and people) and can easily be handled as a specific assignment/request.

With this approach, you would examine the "Top 10" Cost Reduction areas and On-going Cost Controls and decide on which ones you want to attack. You would then assign it to a BoD member, Management Company Agent, Committee member, or other association volunteer to develop a proposed course of action. The back-up information contained on each of these cost reduction areas will quickly orient the responsible party and point them in the right direction. They in turn would present their recommendations to the BoD who will act upon them.

To expand upon specifics of how this approach is used, the following is a step-by-step description of what you should do.

1. INITIATE THE COST REDUCTION EFFORT

The impetus for initiating a cost reduction effort generally is the outcome of a BoD discussion on the state of the association finances. Ultimately, someone says something like, "We have to do something!" or "What should we do to respond to our deteriorating financial condition?" Someone usually takes control and suggests that the association "tighten the belt" by exploring ways to reduce its costs. By default this would be the Treasurer or President, but it could be any BoD member.

At this point, the BoD may not know exactly where to concentrate its efforts. Rather than deciding what to do right then and there, a better approach would be to delay that decision and ask the BoD to arm themselves with some additional knowledge and put some thought into how they might proceed. They should each read through this guide to get a feel for what might possible and what would be involved. Then at their next BoD meeting, they should decide how they would like to proceed.

2. DEFINE THE PROBLEM

If the BoD decides to embark upon a cost reduction effort, there are a couple of things it should do before it actually begins to work on it. First, is to make sure that the BoD understands the problem and its level of severity. Since all problems have solutions, it's critical that you define your problem correctly. If you don't, you might solve the wrong problem. It has been said that "A problem well defined is a problem half solved." Every association will be different, so you will have to make sure that you can clearly articulate what you are trying to fix. A sample problem statement is shown below:

> *Problem Areas*
> *The cost structure for the ABC Association can not continue to support the current level of member services and amenities, without increasing monthly fees or charging a special assessment.*
>
> *It is expected that the association will experience a ___% shortfall in the current year and a ___% shortfall the following year. Unless this can be reversed, members can expect to pay additional monthly fees of*

$_____ or be assessed $_____ in the future. Major areas of cost increases that have been experienced over the past ___ years include:

- *Utilities (___%)*
- *Insurance (___%)*
- *Landscaping (___%)*
- *Maintenance (___%)*

Additional increases are anticipated in future years due to inflation, aging facilities, rising energy costs, and increased wages. Passing along these increased costs without offsetting cost reductions will have several negative consequences on the health and viability of our association

3. STATE THE GOAL

The next thing the BoD should do is to identify the goal of the cost reduction effort by writing a goal statement. The goal statement should be the driving force behind the project. It should be the standard against which everything done on the project is measured. Without a goal, a BoD will not know if it has gone far enough in its cost reduction effort. It may need to go further and make deeper cuts. Shown below is an example project goal statement:

Project Goal
Achieve a ___% reduction in total annual operating costs to the association by _____, without a substantive reduction in member services or amenities.

4. IDENTIFY THE TARGETED COST REDUCTION AREAS

Once the BoD has identified the extent of their financial problems and what it would like to achieve, it is now time to turn their attention to the specific changes they should make to reduce their costs.

As previously mentioned, the place to start is with the Top 10 cost reduction areas. The BoD should identify which of these areas it wishes to pursue for cost reduction opportunity. A quick look at the high cost budget items will usually be a good indicator of which areas will offer the highest rate of return. Ultimately, it also must determine what, if any, changes it would like to make to its on-going cost controls.

5. DETERMINE WHO WILL DO THE WORK

In this step, the BoD should identify the person who will be responsible for assessing and recommending changes to a particular area of association cost that has been targeted for reduction. This person may do it alone or with the help of other project participants. A natural would be a committee chairperson who has some responsibilities for a particular area. For example, the Maintenance & Repair Committee Chairperson would lead the cost reduction effort for the "utilities" section. Available resources (time, money, and people) will usually limit the number of possibilities that can be worked on at once.

Once identified, it would be up to this person to make recommendations to the BoD. Their recommendation should be in written form, using the template shown in Appendix B.

6. SANCTION THE EFFORT AND MAKE ASSIGNMENTS

The next step is for the BoD to give their approval to proceed and to launch the project. It should make the assignments and establish a due date for when the recommendations should come back to the BoD. Depending on association By-Laws, proper decision making procedures should be followed and documented accordingly.

7. MAKE COST REDUCTION DECISIONS

At a designated BoD meeting, each responsible person should present their recommendations to the Board. The BoD will discuss the recommendations and decide to accept, reject, or modify them. It should determine if the recommended actions solve the problem and achieve the stated goal. If not, they may have to go deeper into the well for more cost reductions.

8. IMPLEMENT THE DECISIONS

If the template in Appendix B was used, it identified several things that will aid in the implementation effort, including:

- The next 3-5 high level steps that should be taken to implement the recommended action?
- Who will primarily be responsible for implementing the recommended action?
- When should the recommended action be completed?
- Where should the recommended action occur?

If it was not used, then these items should be identified by the BoD. The BoD should include a progress report at each BoD meeting until the cost reduction efforts have been completed.

COMPREHENSIVE IMPLEMENTATION APPROACH

Some associations will find themselves in a deep financial crisis that requires drastic actions. It may not be enough to just focus on a few of the high cost budget items, using the No-Frills Approach. A more comprehensive approach may be required. With the approach presented in this chapter, you would examine all candidate areas suggested for cost reduction possibility. It is an organization wide effort that leaves no stone unturned and offers the most potential for cost reduction.

It follows a rigorous implementation process that is very common in the business world called project management. It is a disciplined process that defines what steps must be taken and in what sequence, in order to achieved a desired outcome. In our case, this desired outcome or "deliverable" is reduced condo or homeowner association costs.

It uses a tree structure, which is a way of showing the hierarchical nature of all the steps involved in the implementation process.   It is named a "tree structure" because it looks a bit like a tree, even thought this tree is shown sideways compared with a real tree. By looking at this tree structure, you can quickly "see" the major steps that will be taken. It is just another way of summarizing information, but in this case, it is a visual summary.

Shown below is a visual high level summary (tree structure) of how the comprehensive implementation approach is organized. These are the eight major steps that you will take with this approach. You will notice that they are written as an action statement and are broken down into separate pieces of work, which means that ultimately someone has to do something. Subsequent chapters in this guide are then organized around each of these major steps and provide the next level of detail. Tree structures can be an excellent tool to help create understanding and to communicate project implementation specifics in a very condensed format.

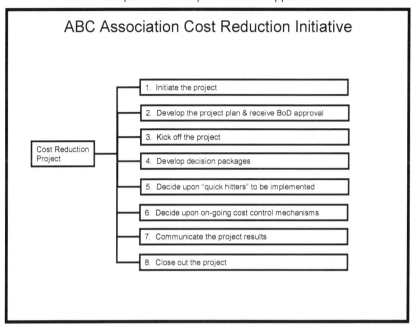

It should be noted that although the following sections tell you exactly what to do under this comprehensive implementation approach, it is not cast in concrete. If you don't like something that is offered, then change it or don't do it. Use you judgment and customize it to fit your unique needs.

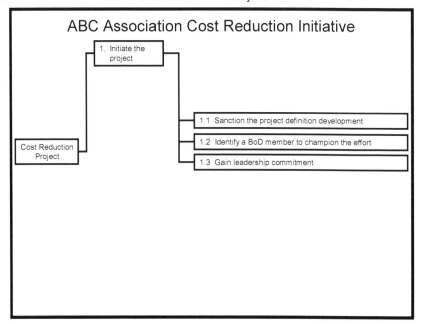

1. INITIATE THE PROJECT

The impetus for initiating a cost reduction effort generally is the outcome of a BoD discussion on the state of the association finances. Ultimately, someone says something like, "We have to do something!" or "What should we do to respond to our deteriorating financial condition?" Hand wringing or blank stares will not help solve this problem. Someone needs to take control and suggest that the association "tighten the belt" by initiating a concentrated cost reduction effort. By default this would be the Treasurer or President, but it could be any BoD member.

At this point, the BoD probably knows little about how the association would go about executing such a project. Rather than deciding what to do right then and there, a better approach would be to delay that decision and ask the BoD to arm themselves with some additional knowledge and put some thought into how they might proceed. So, the following homework assignment should be given to each BoD member for the next meeting:

- Read through this guide to get a feel for what might be possible and what would be involved.
- Prepare yourself to discuss this topic by making some preliminary mental decisions on how you think you should proceed on the following:
  - Do you want to pursue a cost reduction effort and/or an on-going cost control effort?
  - Who will lead the effort?
  - Who will be involved in the effort?
  - What are the BoD expectations, in terms of results, for this effort?
  - What are the timing requirements for this effort?
  - Is there anything "off limits" for this effort?
  - Etc.

Then, at the next BoD meeting, there are three things that you will want to accomplish (outcomes).

1.1. Sanction the Project Definition Development

Open discussions on the above homework assignment will help the BoD begin to formulate some of the expectations and boundaries of any cost reduction project that is to be initiated. It also begins to develop a "shared vision" among the leaders that is needed to drive a successful project. The decision before the BoD is whether or not they should embark upon a focused cost reduction effort and proceed with the next step, which essentially authorizes the development of the project plan specifics.

1.2. Identify A BoD Member To Champion The Effort

Next, the BoD must identify who will lead the effort. In order for any cost reduction effort to be successful, it must have a designated leader or

"Champion." You need someone who will take ownership -- someone to build support/enthusiasm, to organize the activity and to help drive it to a successful conclusion. It is important that this person be a member of the BoD to assure that it receives the necessary clout and access to the top leadership and decision makers.

Generally, a Champion is the person with the passion, technical skill, and commitment to lead the association down this cost reduction path. This obviously requires that the Champion be more than just a cheerleader. This person must have a good understanding of the association, its problems/issues, and its inner workings. This person acts as a teacher to the association, facilitator of improvement efforts, and negotiator when internal organizational issues arise. In most cases, the BoD Champion is the association Treasurer.

The BoD Champion will develop the initial proposal (project plan) for the cost reduction effort and present it to the BoD for approval. However, in some situations, an association's Management Company Agent may be requested to perform this task, under the guidance and direction of the BoD Champion.

1.3. Gain Leadership Commitment

Finally, the BoD must have the proper level of personal commitment from its leaders and key stakeholders. This includes the BoD members and Management Company, if one is used. It is particularly important that they all recognize the need for change and that operating with the status quo is not acceptable. They must further understand that with any change effort, things will be different and that they can expect resistance to any changes that are made. By "committing" to this effort they agree to be actively involved in it and not just supporting it from a distance. They will have to put in the necessary time and effort to bear the fruit they are looking for.

This topic of "commitment" should be discussed among the BoD members and each should verbally state that they intend to fully support this project. Depending on your association By-Laws, it may be necessary to put the measure to a vote before proceeding.

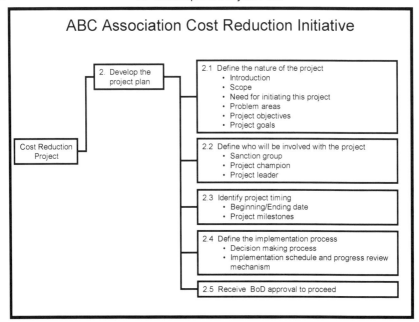

2. DEVELOP THE PROJECT PLAN

Now, that a Champion has been commissioned, it is time for him/her to develop the project plan specifics that will define what is to be done, how it is to be done, by whom, and when.

It is vital that everyone understands and agrees to the plan and "ground rules" that will govern the project from here on in. You need to ensure that the objectives are clearly stated so that there is no disagreement later on. The project plan helps you to control and measure your progress and it will help to cement stakeholder support over the coming months and years of the project.

Your plan should be written and well documented, as it will be used to communicate to several audiences. The time and effort spent developing this document will be a huge time-saver when explaining to others and building support. It will force you to think through exactly what you are looking for and what you are willing to do. It will get everyone involved on the same page and it will lay the foundation for achieving the results that you have targeted. The discussions during the previous BoD meeting should provide an excellent resource for developing this document.

The following sections describe each element of the project plan and provide you with sample wording that may be used. It builds upon itself and in the end; you will have an example of a full project plan. If you like, you can view this completed sample plan first (See *Appendix A*).

2.1. Define the Nature of the Project

The nature of the project defines the project, sets the boundaries, defines what is and what is not in, explains why it is needed, and establishes the goals and objectives. It is made up from several pieces:

2.1.1.   Project Introduction

The project introduction orients the reader to the project being initiated and provides some key background information. It briefly describes the conditions that let to the project and why it is being initiated and by whom. Shown below is a sample project introduction.

Project Introduction
Like many companies, the current economic environment has taken a toll on the financial condition of our association. Rising costs dictate that we react to this situation by increasing fees, reducing services, and/or cut costs. In a recent BoD meeting, the members discussed this growing problem and decided to take a more aggressive approach to cutting our costs and eliminating waste. As a result, we will embark upon a focused and concentrated cost reduction effort over the next several months. The material contained in this package will help you understand the project details, participant responsibilities, and timing requirements.

2.1.2.   Project Scope

Those working on the project must have a common understanding as to what is included in, or excluded from, this cost reduction project. Anyone who has ever done a project will have tales of how scope changes caused grief. It is therefore important to carefully define these boundaries to avoid unnecessary work and effort. This will also keep the project focused and not allow it to wander into areas, such as solving the world's problems.

To help you define your scope, you should answer the following questions:

- Do you want to pursue an immediate cost reduction effort, an on-going cost control effort, or both?
- What association costs are included in the scope of our project? What association costs are NOT included in the scope of the project?
- What association processes are included in the scope of the project? What association processes are NOT included in the scope of the project?

Once you have answered these questions, you should construct a statement for the project scope. An example is shown below.

Project Scope
The BoD is commissioning a cost reduction effort for the association. Broadly, it is trying to eliminate all unnecessary costs -- both discretionary (special projects, landscaping, Management Company, etc.) and non-discretionary (insurance, utilities, taxes, etc.) The primary focus is on 'waste elimination' without sacrificing the quality of member services or amenities. However, changes in member services and/or amenities may occur, particularly if the return does not justify the expense or if it is needed to meet the overall cost reduction objectives for the association. Items that require a change in association governing documents are within scope and may be considered.

At this time, ten areas will be studied for immediate cost reduction savings including:

- *Arrear payment collection*
- *Management Company Services*
- *Administration*
- *Utilities*
- *Insurance*
- *Purchased materials & services*
- *Litigation*
- *Preventative maintenance*
- *Reserve funding*
- *Taxes*

Additionally, several additional areas will be examined to help strengthen the on-going cost controls for future association expenses. They include:

- *Financial management*
- *Financial risk management*

The remaining cost areas and business processes are not considered to be high potential candidates and therefore will not be involved in this effort. Also, measures that may increase association revenue will not be included.

Several people will be involved in studying and eventually recommending a course of action to be taken to improve our cost picture for each of these items. The BoD will make the final decision on all recommendations.

2.1.3.   Need For Initiating This Project

This information is beneficial to project participants to help them understand what perceived need led to this cost reduction effort. Why has the BoD chosen to address it in this manner? Why not use the same approach to reducing costs as has been used in the past? What do you expect to achieve? Why not just hop right in and get to work? These are legitimate questions that should be answered and included in the project plan package. Shown below in an example:

Need For Initiating the Project

Past attempts to reduce and control association costs have been largely fragmented and confined to individual cost items. Most of the attention has been through the efforts of BoD members, who have many other priorities competing for their time. In some cases, increased association expenses were covered with increase fees. Unfortunately, "cost creep" can sneak up on you very quickly. Small incremental increases don't seem like much at the time, but over the long haul and when added collectively, they have added substantial amounts to our cost structure.

A cost reduction project such as this, allows us to systemically examine our major cost items and to make necessary adjustments. It focuses energy and sends a signal to all association members that changes have to be made. Tight timing guidelines create a sense of urgency to assure these things are not studied to death and that we act quickly. It also allows us to expand the involvement of others for short periods of time to help figure out how we can get the biggest bang for the buck! It is felt that an organized and concentrated cost reduction project effort is the most efficient way to drive out waste and unnecessary costs to our association.

2.1.4.   Problem Areas

Since all problems have solutions, it's critical that you define your problem correctly. If you don't, you might solve the wrong problem. It has been said that "A problem well defined is a problem half solved."   Every association will be different, so you will have to make sure that you can clearly articulate what you are trying to fix. Some diagnostic questions include:

- Where is the pain? Are you sure it is a problem? Is it important? What would happen if the "problem" were left alone?
- Where is the problem? Is it an individual cost item or many? Can the association do something about it?
- Why is it a problem? Is there a "gap" between the actual performance and desired performance? For whom is it a problem and why?
- Can the problem be solved permanently or will it occur again? Is this problem masking a deeper systematic problem?

- How urgent is the problem? How important is the problem relative to other problems?
- How high are the stakes?

Shown below is an example problem statement.

Problem Areas
The cost structure for the ABC Association can not continue to support the current level of member services and amenities, without increasing monthly fees or charging a special assessment.

It is expected that the association will experience a ___% shortfall in the current year and a ___% shortfall the following year. Unless this can be reversed, members can expect to pay additional monthly fees of $_____ or be assessed $_____ in the future. Major areas of cost increases that have been experienced over the past ___ years include:

- *Utilities (___%)*
- *Insurance (___%)*
- *Landscaping (___%)*
- *Maintenance (___%)*

Additional increases are anticipated in future years due to inflation, aging facilities, rising energy costs, and increased wages. Passing along these increased costs without offsetting cost reductions will have several negative consequences on the health and viability of our association including:

- *For members currently experiencing financial distress, additional fees will add to their problem, which could increase non-payments, late payments, and foreclosure rates. This will in turn, shift payment responsibility to other association members and the "death spiral" will continue.*
- *Property values will decline and the association could price itself out of the market, due to high maintenance fees. This will then make it more difficult for association members to sell their property, including those that are financially stressed.*
- *A healthy financial condition has to be the top priority for our association. We can not survive if we don't have enough income to pay our bills. We will be forced to cut services and, amenities, expose ourselves to more risks, and take other drastic actions. It is important that we act now while we still have some time!*

2.1.5.   Project Objectives

Project objectives are the concrete statements that describe the specific actions that will be taken to solve the problem and meet the goal. A project objective should be written so that it can be evaluated at the conclusion of a project to see whether it was achieved. Generally, the project is considered to be successful if the project objectives are met successfully. There should be 3-5 project objectives. Shown below is an example project objective statement:

Project Objectives
- *To scrutinize the costs associated with the major expense items of the association and look for reduction opportunities.*
- *To reduce costs primarily through waste elimination and without the need to compromise desired member services or amenities.*
- *To retain only services and amenities required by law or valued by the overwhelming majority of association members.*
- *To engage a broad participation of association members, beyond the BoD, to help determine what is possible.*

2.1.6.   Project Goals

The project goal statement should be the driving force behind the project. It should be the standard against which everything done on the project is measured. A good project goal statement uses the SMART format.

- Specific - The goal should state exactly what the project is to accomplish. It should be phrased using action words (such as "design," "build," "implement," etc.). It should be limited to those essential elements of the project that communicate the purpose of the project and the outcome expected.
- Measurable - If you can't measure it, you can't manage it. In the broadest sense, the whole goal statement is a measure for the project; if the goal is accomplished, the project is a success.

- Agreed-upon – The BoD needs to agree that the project is necessary along with the degree of improvement that is required. Measurable goals that are in agreement with the BoD prevents some from thinking "tweaking" while others are thinking "major overhaul."

- Realistic - This is not a synonym for "easy." Realistic, in this case, means "do-able." It means that the learning curve is not a vertical slope; that the skills needed to do the work are available. It is advisable that a goal contains a considerable amount of "stretch." Otherwise, you may never know what is possible. In a more severe situation where an association's very survival is at risk, it may be necessary to make huge reductions (i.e. – 20%-60%) that cut into the muscle and bone of the organization. You must do what you have to and in that case, "do-able" takes on a dramatically different meaning.

- Time-framed - Probably one of the easiest parts of the goal to establish the deadline. Very little is ever accomplished without a deadline. This is particularly true of work that is in addition to everything else that you need to do in your day. Building the delivery deadline into the project goal keeps it in front of the team members and lets the organization know when they can expect to see the results.

Shown below is an example project goal statement:

Project Goal
Achieve a ___% annual reduction in total operating costs to the association by _____, without a substantive reduction in member services or amenities.

2.2. Define Who Will Be Involved With the Project

This section describes the management oversight that will guide the project along with some of the roles & responsibilities of the people who will be involved.

2.2.1.   Sanction Group

This is always the association BoD members. They serve as the approval group for any recommended actions. They have the authority to accept, reject, or modify anything brought before them. Shown below is an example statement.

Sanction Group
The ABC Association Board of Directors is the approval group for this project. They have final decision making authority on all recommended actions

2.2.2.   Project Champion

In order for any cost reduction effort to be successful, it requires a BoD "Champion." The Project Champion is responsible for directing the project's resources; developing the project plan; communicating the project intent, status, and results, and ensuring that the project is completed on time, within budget, and with acceptable quality. The Champion also plays a primary role interfacing and coordinating with the BoD. Shown below is an example statement.

Project Champion
(_____) has been designated as the Project Champion with the following responsibilities:
- *Establishes objectives, timing and overall project plan*
- *Sets priority and direction for the project*
- *Monitors, evaluates, and tracks progress of the project*
- *Gives assignments to project participants*
- *Serves as the linkage to the BoD Sanction Group*
- *Develops and delivers communications on the project intent, status, and results*
- *Is ultimately responsible for the project quality and output*

2.2.3.   Project Leader (s)

A project Team Leader is the person responsible for assessing and recommending changes to a particular area of association cost that has been targeted for reduction. This person may do it alone or with the help of other project participants. A natural Team Leader would be a committee chairperson who has some responsibilities for a particular area. For example, the Maintenance & Repair Committee Chairperson would lead the cost reduction effort for the "utilities" section. Shown below is an example statement.

Project Team Leader
Project Team Leaders have been identified to help assess and make recommended changes to a particular area of association cost that has been targeted for reduction or improvement. This person may solicit the help of other association members who may be willing to provide assistance.

Targeted Area of Reduction/Improvement	Project Team Leader
Arrear payment collection	
Management Company Services	
Administration	
Utilities	
Insurance	
Purchased materials & services	
Litigation	
Preventative maintenance	
Reserve funding	
Taxes	
Other	
Financial management	
Financial Risk Management	

The responsibilities of the Team Leader are described below for their area of responsibility:
- *Meet project objectives and timing requirements and follow the lead of the Project Champion*
- *Thoroughly research the current conditions*
- *Explore cost reduction alternatives*
- *Decide upon the best action(s) to be taken*

- *Document recommendations on the forms provided and rank order in order of importance*
- *Present recommend changes to the BoD for a final decision*

2.3. Identify Project Timing

This section describes some of the important dates and timing information associated with the project. It is intended to give the project a defined life, with a specific starting and ending point. This helps create a sense of urgency and assures that this project does not create a life of its own where it is studied to death with nothing accomplished. It also provides a timing overview of completion dates for significant events, called milestones. This is useful information to project participants to help them gage the amount of their time that is being committed and when their assignment must be completed.

2.3.1. Beginning/Ending Date

Projects should have a specific beginning and ending date to help create a sense of urgency and to set limits on how long it is expected to exist. Shown below is an example statement.

Beginning/Ending Date
The "ABC Association Cost Reduction Project" is commissioned to start on (month/date/year) and will last through (month/date/year.) It is anticipated that the project participants will support this effort through that time period.

2.3.2. Project Milestones

A milestone is a significant event in the project, usually completion of a major deliverable. Milestones help track progress and determine if the project is on track to finish as expected. For Project Leaders, they are short-term goals which are far more tangible than the distant completion of the entire project. The milestones maintain the momentum and encourage effort. The high level work breakdown structure provides an excellent framework for project milestones. Shown below is an example statement.

Project Milestones

Event or Deliverable	Target Date	Responsibility
Initiate the project	*(insert date)*	*BoD*
Develop the project plan & receive BoD approval	*(insert date)*	*Project Champion*
Kick off the project	*(insert date)*	*Project Champion*
Develop decision packages	*(insert date)*	*Project Leader*
Decide upon "quick hitters" to be implemented	*(insert date)*	*BoD*
Decide upon on-going cost control mechanisms	*(insert date)*	*BoD*
Communicate the project results	*(insert date)*	*Project Champion/BoD*
Close out the project	*(insert date)*	*BoD*

2.4. Define the Implementation Process

The implementation process translates the project into an action plan, with all the details needed by both decision-makers, who will have to commit to the investment of resources, and those charged with carrying it out. It describes the approach that will be taken to bring about the desired change. Ultimately, it is up to the BoD to decide upon which recommendations will be accepted, rejected, or sent back for further study. This is typically handled in a normal BoD meeting; however a special meeting could also be scheduled for this purpose. Shown below is a sample implementation process, which is also the recommended process to be followed by this guide.

Implementation Process

The implementation process translates the project into an action plan, with all the details needed by both decision-makers, who will have to commit to the investment of resources, and those charged with carrying it out. It describes the approach that will be taken to bring about the desired change.

The actual BoD decisions will be made in a designated meeting of the BoD members and project participants (Project Champion and Team Leaders)

Prior to the meeting

Team members will develop a decision package that summarizes their recommended action. A sample can be seen in Appendix B.

During The Meeting

The BoD will make decisions on recommendations to be presented by the Team Leaders. Generally, they will decide to accept, reject, or modify the recommendations.

In the first part of the meeting the BoD will examine the "quick hitter" recommendations and in the second part, it will examine the "on-going cost control" recommendations. Team Leaders will personally present their recommendations to the Board for consideration according the process described below:

Decision Making Process

Team Leaders will arrange their stacked prioritized decision packages on a table or on a wall. If all the recommended Top 10 cost reductions areas are being examined, then there would be 10 piles. (See below)

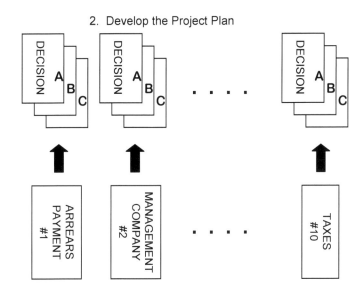

Round #1 - The Team Leaders, one-by-one, will present their top recommendation to the BoD. In the example above, the BoD will choose the top recommendation to accept among the 10 choices. This will then be recorded on a tally sheet to keep track of proper resource utilization and to assure that all the work can be accomplished in a given timeframe. This tally sheet (See Appendix C) can also them be used to track future implementation status. If there are any recommendations that should be rejected on the basis of merit, then the BoD should remove that Team Leader's top choice from the pile. Once round one is completed, you should have 10 piles (or less); again with the top remaining recommendation on the top of each.

Round #2 – The BoD will now compare the top choices from the remaining piles and decide the next one to accept and fund within any given resource, budget, or timing constraints. In the example below, it can be seen that the top choice for pile #1 (Arrear payment collection) was selected in the prior round, therefore their recommendation "B" becomes their top choice in round #2.

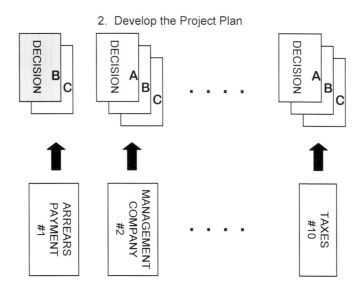

Subsequent rounds – the same process is repeated until all recommendations have been addressed or we run out of resources, funds, or time.

<u>*Implementation schedule*</u>

Once the BoD has made some decisions about reducing its association cost structure, it will finalize the implementation schedule. The cost reduction project "tally sheet" will be beneficial in this regard as it has already documented decisions that were made, the expected completion date, and the person responsible for taking the lead on its implementation. The BoD should now balance the total implementation plan by comparing against the available people, funding, and timing to test for sufficiency. It may have to move some of the recommended implementation dates around, assign lead implementation responsibilities to other people, or free up money in order to balance it with the available resources.

<u>*Progress review mechanism*</u>

A progress review mechanism is needed to assure that the implementation is on track. The project "tally sheet" will serve that purpose. It should be periodically reviewed at a BoD meeting. The BoD should compare the expected results against the actual results and then act accordingly to keep the implementation plans on track.

2.5. Receive BoD Approval to Proceed

Once the project plan has been completed, the next step is for the BoD Champion to review it with the BoD and receive their approval to begin developing the specific cost reduction proposals. Depending on association By-Laws, proper decision making procedures should be followed and documented accordingly

Prior to the meeting, the Champion should forward the BoD a copy of the plan so that they can thoroughly review it. Again, a full sample project plan can be viewed in *Appendix A.*

An optional step that you might want to consider before requesting a decision by the BoD is called "nemawashi." Nemawashi is the Japanese practice of informally sounding out people's ideas about a project or a course of action before a formal proposal is drawn up. When practiced before a meeting, nemawashi ensures that when members meet in person, the group will exhibit consensus rather than disagreement. The way it works is that before the meeting in which you make a formal proposal, you discuss it with other BoD members to obtain their views and initial reactions. This is the time to build support for the project, to identify any "blind spots" or holes that you may have missed, and to gather information that may be critical for a successful implementation. This informal discussion allows for people to discuss their true feelings, including those who may have strong objections to the project, or others who may have new ideas.

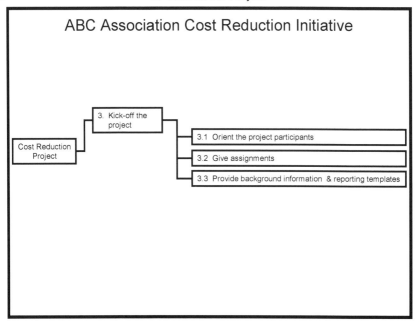

3. KICK-OFF THE PROJECT

Upon BoD approval, you can now hold a Project Kick-off Meeting, which formally recognizes the start of the project. It should involve the BoD members and the people who will be participating in the project. During this meeting, you want to energize the group and build momentum. There are several other things you want to accomplish as well, including:

- Demonstrate to your team that you are organized and have a well thought out plan.
- Explain each team member's responsibilities and give assignments to those who will be recommending changes.
- Encourage all to help one another and to be accountable to the project. Everyone pulling together for a common cause can have dramatic results.
- Provide next steps and timing. Team members should have a clear understanding of what they have to do and by when.

3.1. Orient the Project Participants

Since you have completed your project plan, you have all the materials you need to run this meeting and to orient those participants who will be involved with the project. Essentially, you will review the plan and then allow team members to discuss it and ask questions.

3.2. Give Assignments

The Team Leaders should be given their assignments and their roles and responsibilities should be reviewed with them. It is important that they completely understand their assignment, the expectations, and the timing requirements.

3.3. Provide Background Information and Reporting Templates

At this meeting each Team Leader should be given a Team Leader instruction package (*See sample in Appendix D*) that includes:

- Explanation of their assignment, the expectations of them as a Team Leader, and their deliverables
- Important background information for their particular area of focus along with the forms and templates that are to be used
- Suggestions on how to proceed with their assignment
- Instructions on how to create a decision package

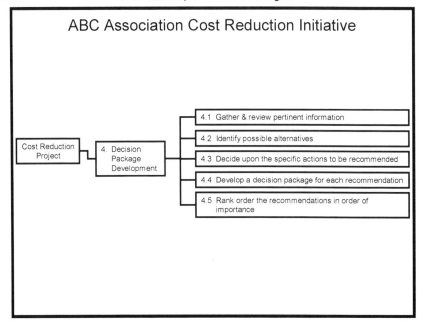

4. DEVELOP DECISION PACKAGES

Now that everyone has been oriented and assignments have been given to the Team Leaders, it is time for them to begin their work. The major deliverable or output for each project Team Leader is a recommendation on how to reduce association cost for their assigned area of concentration.

Detailed instructions for approaching their assignment and developing a decision package are described below. This Team Leader Instructions information should be provided to the Team Leader during the kick-off meeting.

4.1. Define the Problem/Opportunity

This is often where people struggle. They react to what they think the problem is. Instead, seek to understand more about why you think there's a problem. Ask yourself and others, the following questions:

- What can you see that causes you to think there's a problem/opportunity?
- Where is it happening?
- How is it happening?
- When is it happening?
- With whom is it happening?
- Why is it happening?
- Write down a clean and succinct description of the problem/opportunity in terms of "The following should be happening, but isn't ..." or "The following is happening and should be: ..." As much as possible, be specific in your description, including what is happening, where, how, with whom and why.

4.2. Identify Causes of the Problem/Pertinent Information

It's amazing how much you don't know about what you don't know. Therefore, in this step, it's critical that you write down key bits of information that may open up or constrain a potential solution. It is here that you also identify all of the possible causes of the problem in terms of what is happening, where, when, how, with whom and why. Talk to people who are experiencing the problem for their ideas and suggestions. Consult with experts in the field to get their opinions. Thoroughly research your focus area to assure that you are well versed in what may or may not be possible.

4.3. Identify alternatives

At this point, you should now brainstorm for solutions to the problem/opportunity. Very simply put, brainstorming is collecting as many ideas as possible. It's critical when collecting the ideas to not pass any judgment on the ideas -- just write them down as they come to mind or you hear them.   Look for clues on how a cost can be eliminated or reduced including:

- Can the product or service be eliminated, reduced, or reconfigured?
- What things we should continue doing, start doing, stop doing?
- Why do we have this cost?
- Do we need this cost?
- What are some different ways to do what we have been doing?
- Are we being charged the proper amount for this service?
- What is the price of this service? Why?
- How do we know our price for this service is competitive?
- What are other associations paying for this service? Why are we paying more? How do we know we are being charged the proper amount? Can we share costs?
- Can we redesign the product or process to eliminate the cost entirely?
- Can we change the specs to reduce the costs to the vendor supplying the goods or service?
- Can we standardize the specifications or change the delivery schedule to increase volume buying capability.
- When was the last time this price was negotiated?
- Can we buy this product or service from someone else?
- Can we outsource this service?
- What can I take away? What is barely sufficient?
- Have I made the best use of technology or new products?

4.4. Select the best alternative(s)

As you brainstorm possible solutions, some clear candidates for action should begin to surface. There may be more than one best alternative or action that you could take. When selecting the best alternative, consider:

- Which alternative is the most likely to solve the problem or capitalize on the opportunity for the long term?
- Which alternative is the most realistic to accomplish for now?
- Do we have the resources? Are they affordable? Do we have enough time to implement the alternative?
- What is the extent of risk associated with each alternative?
- Can two or more alternatives be combined into a stronger one?

4.5. Plan the implementation

Once you have made a decision on the best alternative(s), you should identify some of the initial steps that should be taken to implement the recommended action. Use the What?, Who?, When?, and Where? question format.

- What are the next 3-5 high level steps that should be taken to implement the recommended action?
- Who will primarily be responsible for implementing the recommended action?
- When should the recommended action be completed?
- Where should the recommended action occur?

4.6. Create Your Decision Package(s)

A decision package (See *Appendix B*) organizes and describes a proposed cost reduction recommendation in a very condensed

fashion. It consolidates the recommended action, background
information, supporting justification, and the statement of impact.
Summarizing it in writing allows the BoD to quickly come up to the
recommender's knowledge level and the rationale that was used for
the proposed recommendation. Its 1-page format provides a
standardized way to display the critical information and for the BoD
to compare competing projects where resources are limited.

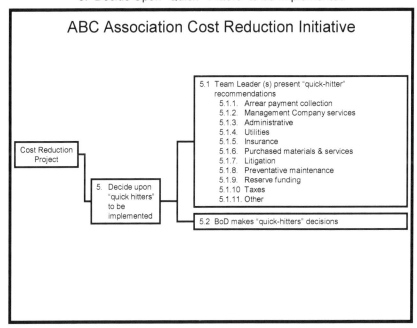

5. DECIDE UPON "QUICK-HITTERS" TO BE IMPLEMENTED

The decision packages completed by the Team Leaders provide the mechanism for the BoD to decide upon which actions they will take to reduce their cost structure. The Project Champion should make arrangements for a meeting that would involve the BoD, Team Leaders, and anyone else deemed to be appropriate. In order to gain the quickest cost reduction benefit with the least amount of effort the BoD will want to first focus upon the "quick-hitters" -- the Top 10 cost-saving return areas of opportunity (See *Appendix E*). This low-hanging fruit is highly visible, easily obtained, and provides immediate opportunities for cost reduction. Furthermore, it can generate interest, support, and momentum for more ambitious initiatives.

5.1. Team Leader (s) Present "Quick-Hitter" Recommendations

5. Decide Upon "Quick –Hitters" to be Implemented

Each Team Leader Team will present their prioritized "quick hitter" decision packages to the BoD for a decision, according to the implementation process discussed earlier.

5.2. BoD Makes "Quick-Hitter" Decisions

The BoD will choose the top recommendation to accept among the recommendations being made by the Team Leaders. This will then be recorded on a tally sheet (*See Appendix C*) to keep track of proper resource utilization and to assure that all the work can be accomplished in a given timeframe.

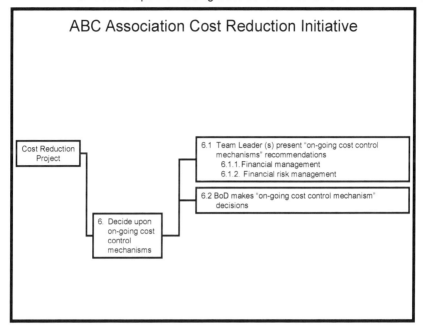

6. DECIDE UPON ON-GOING COST CONTROL MECHANISMS

Now that you have exhausted the Top 10 "quick-hitters", you hopefully have made some significant cost reductions and gained some all important breathing room to focus your attention on preventing unnecessary or inefficient spending from occurring again in the future. These on-going cost controls will help prevent "cost creep" and help eliminate waste at its source. It is time for the BoD to now examine this second group of opportunities.

6.1. Team Leader (s) Present "On-Going Cost Control Mechanisms" Recommendations

Each Team Leader will present their prioritized "on-going cost control mechanism" decision packages to the BoD for a decision.

6.2. BoD Makes "On-Going Cost Control Mechanisms" Decisions

The BoD will choose the top recommendation to accept among the recommendations being made by the Team Leaders. This will then be recorded on a tally sheet (See *Appendix C*) to keep track of proper resource utilization and to assure that all the work can be accomplished in a given timeframe.

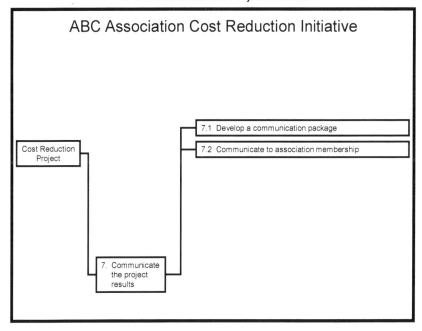

7. COMMUNICATE THE PROJECT RESULTS

Communicating results is a critical issue for the success of any cost reduction project such as this. While it is important to communicate achieved results to interested stakeholders once the project is complete, it is also important to communicate throughout the project. This ensures that information is flowing so adjustments can be made and so that all stakeholders are aware of the success and issues surrounding the project solution implementation.

7.1. Develop A Communications Package

You should carefully craft a staged communications plan (see sample below) that identifies what information will be communicated (new information, progress to date, anticipated problems, decisions made), how it will be communicated (personal contact, letter or email, group meeting), by whom will it be communicated (President, Secretary, all

BoD), and when will it be communicated (date, frequency). You want to give the association members a steady flow of information that addresses the things on their mind along with the things that the BoD wants to communicate to them.

ABC Association Cost Reduction Communication Plan			
What	**How**	**Who**	**When**
PROJECT INITIATION			
Announce to the association membership the initiation of the cost reduction effort and explain: • Nature of the project (including how members will be impacted) • Who will be involved (Project Champion and Team Leaders) • Project timing • Implementation details	President Letter (newsletter, email, website)	BoD President	(Date)
ONGOING COMMUNICATIONS			
Overall progress report to the BoD on • Key findings • Accomplishments thus far • Is the project on track?	(BoD meeting, email)	Project Champion	(Monthly)
(Monthly) Overall progress report to membership on • Key findings • Accomplishments thus far • Is the project on track?	(Newsletter, email, website)	Project Champion/ Secretary	(Monthly)
(As-required) Member input for actions under consideration. • Viewpoints on something particularly expensive or controversial	(Direct contact, newsletter, email, website)	Team Leader	(As-required)
(Whenever possible) Casual	(Direct contact)	BoD/	(Whenever possible)

conversations with membership • Explain project benefits and efforts to association members • Answer questions or address concerns		Project Leader/ Team Leader	
PROJECT COMPLETION			
Announce to the association membership the completion of the cost reduction effort and explain: • Project accomplishments and results • Expected benefits • Expected timing • Expected changes	President Letter (newsletter, email, website)	BoD President	(Date)
Recognize project participant efforts	President Letter (newsletter, email, website)	BoD President	(Date)

7.2. Communicate To Association Membership

As you can see in the sample communication plan, the last item concerns itself with communicating the project results. The reasons for communicating project results depend on the specific project, the setting, and the unique needs. The most common needs for communicating project results include:

• **Recognition.** The people who were instrumental in bring about the desired change should be formally recognized for their efforts. A simple "thank you", pat on the back, or other forms of non-monetary awards should be used extensively. Members who are recognized for their contributions will be even more committed to helping the association meet its cost reduction goals. Recognition shows them that their individual and collective contributions make a difference and are valued. Praise is a very effective motivator.

- **Demonstration of BoD leadership**. By communicating the cost reduction measures that are being taken, a BoD builds confidence and trust with the association members. This is an excellent opportunity to demonstrate how effective the BoD has been in efficiently running an association and its ability to lead.

- **Follow-Up Commitment.** Once you go public with the cost reduction plan, it becomes highly visible with the association membership and it reinforces the commitment to follow through.

- **Member Support.** It is important to have support for the recommended changes by the association BoD and membership. This communication is intended to build the necessary support to help make project solutions successful.

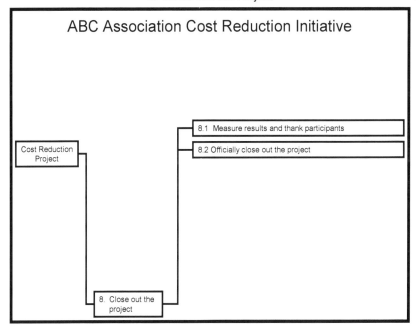

8. CLOSE OUT THE PROJECT

The project close-out finalizes all project activities, except for any on-going activities, and officially brings closure.

8.1. Measure Results and Thank Participants

The purpose of project closeout is to assess the project, ensure completion, and to thank participants. The key elements of project close-out are:

8.1.1. Verify Acceptance Of Final Project Deliverables

The first step of the close-out process is the BoD's acceptance of the final deliverables of the project. This is a critical and important step, because it signifies that the BoD agrees that the scope of the project and its deliverables are complete and were delivered as agreed upon by all parties.

8.1.2.   Recognize and Celebrate Outstanding Project Work

Celebrating the success of completing a project with positive reinforcement can be extremely rewarding for project teams. When a project is completed successfully, be certain to provide some kind of recognition to the team. Recognition can involve:

8.1.2.1.   Openly give praise

The BoD may want to express recognition of a successful team effort by praising the team at a BoD meeting or at the Annual Meeting. People are proud to have a BoD's appreciation openly expressed, and such recognition is a motivation to other projects to be successful.

8.1.2.2.   Grant non-monetary awards

Plaques, mugs, medals, jackets, pen & pencil sets, briefcases, calculators, engraved crystal sculptures, lapel pins, paperweights, notepads, etc. are all examples of non-monetary awards

8.1.2.3.   Celebrate successes

An excellent way to close out the project and recognize contributions is to host a recognition luncheon/dinner for the project participants. The BoD President could formally recognize the efforts of the team and provide a token of appreciation.

8.2. Complete and Archive Final Project Records.

Historic project data is an important source of information to help improve future projects. All records, both electronic and hard copy should be stored according to record retention guidelines. Typically, at a minimum, the following project data is archived:

- Project charter
- Project plan
- Project management control documents
- Correspondence
- Meeting notes
- Status reports

SUMMARY

Leading a condo or homeowner association back to financial health can be a rewarding and challenging experience for any Board of Directors. Ultimately, with costs continuing to rise, they will have to decide if the owner fees should be increased or if amenities and services should be reduced. A more desirable option is to do neither and eliminate spending waste.

An organized cost reduction effort can be a very effective tool in identifying this waste and taking the necessary steps to eliminate it. This guide provides a BoD a detailed plan of attack for implementing such an effort. It incorporates "best practices" from similar business settings in both content and implementation methodology.

While traveling this journey, a responsible Board of Directors will take the actions necessary to ensure the financial health and viability of the association it governs. A systematic examination of all costs coupled with strong and decisive leadership will help reduce your condo or homeowner association costs now and in the future!

Appendix A – Cost Reduction Project Plan

Proposal

ABC Association Cost Reduction Project Plan

Submitted to
Board of Directors

By
Project Champion

On

January 1, XXXX

Purpose

The purpose of this package is to recommend an approach to the Board of Directors (BoD) of the ABC Association on how to reduce its costs now and in the future. BoD approval is being sought to initiate this project and to follow the course of action that is outlined

Project Introduction

Like many companies, the current economic environment has taken a toll on the financial condition of our association. Rising costs dictate that we react to this situation by increasing fees, reducing services, and/or cut costs. In a recent BoD meeting, the members discussed this growing problem and decided to take a more aggressive approach to cutting our costs and eliminating waste. As a result, we will embark upon a focused and concentrated cost reduction effort over the next several months. The material contained in this package will help you understand the project details, participant responsibilities, and timing requirements.

Project Scope

The BoD is commissioning a cost reduction effort for the association. Broadly, it is trying to eliminate all unnecessary costs -- both discretionary (special projects, landscaping, Management Company, etc.) and non-discretionary (insurance, utilities, taxes, etc.) The primary focus is on 'waste elimination' without sacrificing the quality of member services or amenities. However, changes in member services and/or amenities may occur, particularly if the return does not justify the expense or if it is needed to meet the overall cost reduction objectives for the association. Items that require a change in association governing documents are within scope and may be considered.

At this time, ten areas will be studied for immediate cost reduction savings including:

- *Arrear payment collection*
- *Management Company Services*
- *Administration*
- *Utilities*
- *Insurance*
- *Purchased materials & services*
- *Litigation*
- *Preventative maintenance*
- *Reserve funding*
- *Taxes*

Additionally, several additional areas will be examined to help strengthen the on-going cost controls for future association expenses. They include:

- *Financial management*
- *Financial risk management*

The remaining cost areas and business processes are not considered to be high potential candidates and therefore will not be involved in this effort. Also, measures that may increase association revenue will not be included.

Several people will be involved in studying and eventually recommending a course of action to be taken to improve our cost picture for each of these items. The BoD will make the final decision on all recommendations.

Who Will Be Involved With The Project

Several people will be involved in studying and eventually recommending a course of action to be taken to improve our cost picture for each of these items. The BoD will make the final decision on all recommendations

Need For Initiating the Project

Past attempts to reduce and control association costs have been largely fragmented and confined to individual cost items. Most of the attention has been through the efforts of BoD members, who have many other priorities competing for their time. In some cases, increased association expenses were covered with increase fees. Unfortunately, "cost creep" can sneak up on you very quickly. Small incremental increases don't seem like much at the time, but over the long haul and when added collectively, they have added substantial amounts to our cost structure.

A cost reduction project such as this, allows us to systemically examine our major cost items and to make necessary adjustments. It focuses energy and sends a signal to all association members that changes have to be made. Tight timing guidelines create a sense of urgency to assure these things are not studied to death and that we act quickly. It also allows us to expand the involvement of others for short periods of time to help figure out how we can get the biggest bang for the buck! It is felt that an organized and concentrated cost reduction project effort is the most efficient way to drive out waste and unnecessary costs to our association.

Problem Areas

The cost structure for the ABC Association can not continue to support the current level of member services and amenities, without increasing monthly fees or charging a special assessment.

It is expected that the association will experience a ___% shortfall in the current year and a ___% shortfall the following year. Unless this can be reversed, members can expect to pay additional monthly fees of $_____ or be assessed $_____ in the future. Major areas of cost increases that have been experienced over the past ___ years include:

- Utilities (___%)
- Insurance (___%)
- Landscaping (___%)
- Maintenance (___%)

Additional increases are anticipated in future years due to inflation, aging facilities, rising energy costs, and increased wages. Passing along these increased costs without offsetting cost reductions will have several negative consequences on the health and viability of our association including:

For members currently experiencing financial distress, additional fees will add to their problem, which could increase non-payments, late payments, and foreclosure rates. This will in turn, shift payment responsibility to other association members and the "death spiral" will continue.

Property values will decline and the association could price itself out of the market, due to high maintenance fees. This will then make it more difficult for association members to sell their property, including those that are financially stressed.

A healthy financial condition has to be the top priority for our association. We can not survive if we don't have enough income to pay our bills. We will be forced to cut services and amenities, expose ourselves to more risks, and take other drastic actions. It is important that we act now while we still have some time!

Project Objectives

- To scrutinize the costs associated with the major expense items of the association and look for reduction opportunities.
- To reduce costs primarily through waste elimination and without the need to compromise desired member services or amenities.
- To retain only services and amenities required by law or valued by the overwhelming majority of association members.
- To engage a broad participation of association members, beyond the BoD, to help determine what is possible.

Project Goal

Achieve a ___% reduction in total annual operating costs to the association by _____, without a substantive reduction in member services or amenities.

Sanction Group

The ___ Association BoD is the approval group for this project. They have final decision making authority on all recommended actions

Project Champion

(_____) has been designated as the Project Champion with the following responsibilities:

- Establishes objectives, timing and overall project plan
- Sets priority and direction for the project
- Monitors, evaluates, and tracks progress of the project
- Gives assignments to project participants
- Serves as the linkage to the BoD Sanction Group
- Develops and delivers communications on the project intent, status, and results

- Is ultimately responsible for the project quality and output

Project Team Leader

Project Team Leaders have been identified to help assess and make recommended changes to a particular area of association cost that has been targeted for reduction or improvement. This person may solicit the help of other association members who may be willing to provide assistance.

Targeted Area of Reduction/Improvement	*Project Team Leader*
Arrear payment collection	
Management Company services	
Administration	
Utilities	
Insurance	
Purchased materials & services	
Litigation	
Preventative maintenance	
Reserve funding	
Taxes	
Other	
Financial management	
Financial risk management	

The responsibilities of the Team Leader are described below for their area of responsibility:

- Meet project objectives and timing requirements and follow the lead of the Project Champion

- Thoroughly research the current conditions
- Explore cost reduction alternatives
- Decide upon the best action(s) to be taken
- Document recommendations on the forms provided and rank order in order of importance
- Present recommend changes to the BoD for a final decision

Beginning/Ending Date

The "ABC Association Cost Reduction Project" is commissioned to start on (month/date/year) and will last through (month/date/year.) It is anticipated that the project participants will support this effort through that time period.

Project Milestones

Event or Deliverable	Target Date	Responsibility
Initiate the project	(insert date)	BoD
Develop the project plan & receive BoD approval	(insert date)	Project Champion
Kick off the project	(insert date)	Project Champion
Develop decision packages	(insert date)	Project Leader
Decide upon "quick hitters" to be implemented	(insert date)	BoD
Decide upon on-going cost control mechanisms	(insert date)	BoD
Communicate the project results	(insert date)	Project Champion/BoD
Close out the project	(insert date)	BoD

Decision Making Process

Ultimately, it is up to the BoD to decide upon which recommendations will be accepted, rejected, or sent back for further study. This is typically handled in a normal BoD meeting; however a special meeting could also be scheduled for this purpose. In the first part of the meeting the BoD will examine the "quick hitter" recommendations and in the second part, it will examine the "on-going cost control" recommendations. Team Leaders will personally present their recommendations to the Board for consideration according the process described below:

Implementation Process

The implementation process translates the project into an action plan, with all the details needed by both decision-makers, who will have to commit to the investment of resources, and those charged with carrying it out. It describes the approach that will be taken to bring about the desired change.

Team members will develop a decision package that summarizes their recommended action. A sample can be seen below:

Cost-Savings Recommendation for Board of Director's Decision

Issue Title: (Clear and short title)   **Submitted by:** (Submitter's name)   **(#)**
Date: (Submission date)

Ease of Implementation

Financial Impact:

Initial Cost (IC)	
Annual Cost (AC)	
Annual Savings (AS)	
Annual Cost-Savings (ACS) = (AS-AC)	
Payback in years = ((IC÷ACS)	

Payback

	Easy & Quick	Difficult & Longer
Less than 1 yr.	1	3
More than 1 yr.	2	4

Data and Background:
- (List the key facts here that the decision makers should take into account. This should be in executive summary form and should only contain the most pertinent information)

Recommendation:
- (If you were the Board of Directors, what decision would you make? This section should describe the decision is sufficient detail that it can stand on its own.)

Immediate Next Steps	Responsibility	Target Due Date
1.		
2.		
3.		

They will arrange their stacked prioritized decision packages on a table or on a wall. If all the recommended Top 10 cost reductions areas are being examined, then there would be 10 piles. (See below)

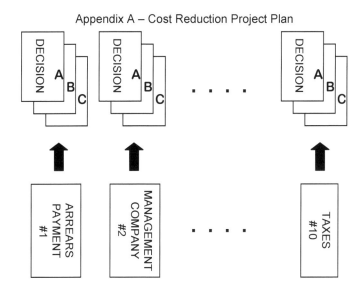

Round #1 - The Team Leaders, one-by-one, will present their top recommendation to the BoD. In the example above, the BoD will choose the top recommendation to accept among the 10 choices. This will then be recorded on a tally sheet to keep track of proper resource utilization and to assure that all the work can be accomplished in a given timeframe. This tally sheet can also be used to track future implementation status. If there are any recommendations that should be rejected on the basis of merit, then the BoD should remove that Team Leader's top choice from the pile. Once round one is completed, you should have 10 piles (or less); again with the top remaining recommendation on the top of each.

Round #2 – The BoD will now compare the top choices from the remaining piles and decide the next one to accept and fund within any given resource, budget, or timing constraints. In the example below, it can be seen that the top choice for pile #1 (Arrear payment collection) was selected in the prior round, therefore their recommendation "B" becomes their top choice in round #2.

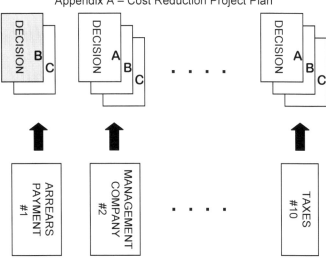

Subsequent rounds – the same process is repeated until all recommendations have been addressed or we run out of resources, funds, or time.

Implementation schedule

Once the BoD has made some decisions about reducing its association cost structure, it will finalize the implementation schedule. The cost reduction project "tally sheet" will be beneficial in this regard as it has already documented decisions that were made, the expected completion date, and the person responsible for taking the lead on its implementation. The BoD should now balance the total implementation plan by comparing against the available people, funding, and timing to test for sufficiency. It may have to move some of the recommended implementation dates around, assign lead implementation responsibilities to other people, or free up money in order to balance it with the available resources.

Progress review mechanism

A progress review mechanism is needed to assure that the implementation is on track. The project "tally sheet" will serve that purpose. It should be periodically reviewed at a BoD meeting. The BoD should compare the expected results against the actual results and then act accordingly to keep the implementation plans on track.

Appendix B – Decision Package

Cost-Savings Recommendation for Board of Director's Decision

Issue Title: (Clear and short title)   **Submitted by:** (Submitter's name)   **(#)**
                                    Date: (Submission date)

Financial Impact:

Initial Cost (IC)	
Annual Cost (AC)	
Annual Savings (AS)	
Annual Cost-Savings (ACS) = (AS-AC)	
Payback in years = ((IC÷ACS)	

Ease of Implementation

Payback	Easy & Quick	Difficult & Longer
Less than 1 yr.	1	3
More than 1 yr.	2	4

Data and Background:
- (List the key facts here that the decision makers should take into account. This should be in executive summary form and should only contain the most pertinent information)

Recommendation:
- (If you were the Board of Directors, what decision would you make? This section should describe the decision is sufficient detail that it can stand on its own.)

Immediate Next Steps	Responsibility	Target Due Date
1.		
2.		
3.		

Appendix C – Tally Sheet

ABC Association

Approved Cost Reduction Actions

Introduction

The following cost reduction measures have been accepted by the BoD and will be implemented according to the following schedule.

Cost Reduction Item Requiring Action	Resp.	Due Date	Cost Estimate	Running Cost Total

Appendix D – Team Leader Instruction Package

ABC Association Cost Reduction Project

Team Leader Instructions

Assignment:

You have been asked to help our association identify cost reduction opportunities through your involvement in a concentrated cost reduction project. As a Team Leader, you will recommend a course of action for reducing association cost in your assigned area of concentration. You will document your recommendation in a "decision package" and present it to the BoD for approval or non-approval.

It should be noted that we would like you to follow the doctrine of "completed staff work", which essentially says that you should present your recommendations in such a form that all that needs to be done by the BoD is to indicate their approval or disapproval. You should advise the BoD what they ought to do, not ask them what you should do. Your recommendation should represent what you would do if you were in the position of a BoD officer for your association.

Ask yourself the following questions to assure that you have met the requirements of completed staff work:

- Have I met the project objectives and goals?
- Are my conclusions supported by specific facts? Are they logical and can I explain the logic?
- Is the recommendation in a finished form?
- Am I presenting a solution rather than a question?
- Am I presenting a single course of action versus several alternatives?

- Can the BoD make the decision on the spot with what I have proposed?
- Have I done all that I could do versus leaving something for the BoD to do?

Important Background Information:

You should have been provided the following background information to help orient you to your assignment. Carefully read the material to assure that you understand the project objectives & goals, Team Leader requirements, background information on your focus area, and alternatives that you may want to consider.

- ABC Association cost reduction project plan
- Team Leader Instructions (this document)
- Focus area background information ("Top Ten" cost reduction areas of opportunity or on-going cost controls)

How to Proceed:

The following is meant to provide you with an organized approach for developing your recommendations. It is a rational approach used to help solve problems and make decisions.

- Define the problem/opportunity
- This is often where people struggle. They react to what they think the problem is. Instead, seek to understand more about why you think there's a problem. Ask yourself and others, the following questions:
- What can you *see* that causes you to think there's a problem/opportunity?
- Where is it happening?

- How is it happening?
- When is it happening?
- With whom is it happening?
- Why is it happening?

Write down a clean and succinct description of the problem/opportunity in terms of "The following should be happening, but isn't ..." or "The following is happening and should be: ..." As much as possible, be specific in your description, including what is happening, where, how, with whom and why.

Identify Possible Causes of the Problem/Pertinent Information:

It's amazing how much you don't know about what you don't know. Therefore, in this step, it's critical that you write down key bits of information that may open up or constrain a potential solution. It is here that you also identify all of the possible causes of the problem in terms of what is happening, where, when, how, with whom and why. Talk to people who are experiencing the problem for their ideas and suggestions. Consult with experts in the field to get their opinions. Thoroughly research your focus area to assure that you are well versed in what many or may not be possible.

Identify alternatives to resolve the problem/capitalize on the opportunity:

At this point, you should now brainstorm for solutions to the problem/opportunity. Very simply put, brainstorming is collecting as many ideas as possible. It's critical when collecting the ideas to not pass any judgment on the ideas -- just write them down as they come to mind or you hear them. Look for clues on how a cost can be eliminated or reduced including:

- Can the product or service be eliminated, reduced, or reconfigured?

- What things we should continue doing, start doing, stop doing?
- Why do we have this cost?
- Do we need this cost?
- What are some different ways to do what we have been doing?
- Are we being charged the proper amount for this service?
- What is the price of this service? Why?
- How do we know our price for this service is competitive?
- What are other associations paying for this service? Why are we paying more? How do we know we are being charged the proper amount? Can we share costs?
- Can we redesign the product or process to eliminate the cost entirely?
- Can we change the specs to reduce the costs to the vendor supplying the goods or service?
- Can we standardize the specifications or change the delivery schedule to increase volume buying capability.
- When was the last time this price was negotiated?
- Can we buy this product or service from someone else?
- Can we outsource this service?
- What can I take away? What is barely sufficient?
- Have I made the best use of technology or new products?

Select the best alternative(s) to resolve the problem/ capitalize on the opportunity:

As you brainstorm for possible solutions, some clear candidates for action should begin to surface. There may be more than one best alternative or actions that you could take. When selecting the best alternative, consider:

- Which alternative is the most likely to solve the problem or capitalize on the opportunity for the long term?
- Which alternative is the most realistic to accomplish for now?

- Do we have the resources? Are they affordable? Do we have enough time to implement the alternative?
- What is the extent of risk associated with each alternative?
- Can two or more alternatives be combined into a stronger one?

Plan the implementation:

Once you have made a decision on the best alternative(s), you should detail the some of the initial steps that should be taken to implement the recommended action. Use the What?, Who?, When?, and Where? question format.

- What are the next 3-5 high level steps that should be taken to implement the recommended action?
- Who will primarily be responsible for implementing the recommended action?
- When should the recommended action be completed?
- Where should the recommended action occur?

Creating Your Decision Package(s):

A decision package organizes and describes a proposed cost reduction recommendation in a very condensed fashion. It consolidates the recommended action, background information, supporting justification, and the statement of impact. Summarizing it in writing allows the BoD to quickly come up to the recommender's knowledge level and the rationale that was used for the proposed recommendation. Its 1-page format provides a standardized way to display the critical information and for the BoD to compare competing projects where resources are limited.

Appendix E – Top 10 Cost-Savings Return Areas of Opportunity

Listed in priority order (highest to lowest cost reduction opportunity)

1. Arrear payment collection

Even though this is technically not a cost category, it should be the first thing an association examines to help remedy its cost problem. It is quick, requires no substantive change in practices, and is always preferred to raising fees or reducing services. Essentially it is collecting the money that is due an association from members who have not paid their fees in a timely fashion. Since this represents a "loan" that is past due, a more aggressive collection approach should be taken to stem losses before the amounts become overwhelming. This can also sends a signal that monthly charges are not something you can let slip.

2. Management Company Services

If and how you use a Management Company to help manage your association duties, will be an important area to examine for cost reduction opportunity. This category of expense can run upwards of 30% of an association's annual budget -- money that you may be able to spend more wisely. Depending on the nature and severity of your financial situation, you may be forced to take on more of those duties even though it may not be your first choice. Elimination of some or all of the services, rebidding/renegotiation of the Management Company contract, innovative use of private contractors or specialty service providers, holding Management Companies more accountable for cost reduction and/or "partnering" to jointly attack cost reduction, are all within the realm of possibilities.

3. Administration

A condo or homeowner association's administrative activities generally involve storing, retrieving, and integrating information for dissemination to association members and the BoD. With recent advances in technologies such as email, web-based services, self-serve pulling of information, electronic requests, automated response systems, auto bill paying and money transfer, inexpensive association websites, document scanning, etc., it offers an excellent opportunity for an association to simultaneously reduce its cost and improve its service.

4. Utilities

Rising energy costs (natural gas, oil, electricity) or increased utility costs (water, sewage, waste removal) are prompting many condo or homeowner associations to analyze their usage and to take steps to reduce or eliminate waste. Depending on the solutions, the payback can be fast or intermediate, with costs ranging from being free to being a long-term investment. Knowing where to focus your attention and how to prioritize are essential to developing an effective, realistic energy/utilities savings plan. Since this can be a major expense for an association, it is a primary area of opportunity for saving current costs and/or heading future costs increases.

5. Insurance

Insurance cost can be one of the biggest costs to a condo or homeowner association. Knowing the specifics of your insurance policy and also being familiar with the property that the policy covers, can save you money now and for many years to come. An important feature to understand is what the individual condo unit owner insurance covers and what the association policy covers in the event of damage. There are several ways in which an association can lower its insurance cost; reduce the insurance liabilities, increase the deductible amount, adopt a policy that the responsible unit owner's insurance will pay the association's deductible, specify that owner's unit insurance will be the primary coverage in the event of duplicate coverage, shop around for a lower price.

6. Purchased materials & services

From time to time you should carefully examine every single purchased service cost you incur. This can include Management Company, landscaping, lawn cutting, irrigation, snow plowing, pool/spa maintenance, property maintenance, attorney, insurance, bookkeeping/accounting, TV/cable, utilities, common area housekeeping, pest control, locksmith, pond control, etc. This examination shouldn't just focus on renegotiating prices or getting more bids.   Rather, it should explore every way possible to reduce the cost or, ideally, eliminate it altogether. You'll find that if you focus on just one item at a time, you'll often be able to come up with some really creative solutions.

7. Litigation

One area often available for pruning is your legal expense that can be kept under control with a few basic strategies. The highest component of any association's legal expenses is litigation and you want to minimize it at almost any cost. It is the area most likely to wreak havoc with the budget because it's so unpredictable and with the high costs for an experienced trial lawyer, litigation can quickly become a sink hole for association dollars. There are also many cost-savings opportunities to minimize the use of an attorney for other more routing aspects of your association's business.

8. Preventative maintenance

There are significant cost-reduction and productivity-improvement opportunities available with a streamlined, proactive approach to the maintenance of an association's physical assets. Preventive maintenance is an essential component that should serve as the core activity to any maintenance plan.   According to a recent report by Jones Lang LaSalle (a global real estate services and money management firm), an organization/association that spends at the industry benchmark level for preventative maintenance will experience a 545% return over time. That is a large return on investment that can not be ignored. Simply put, preventative maintenance is a significant cost effective method of maintaining current equipment or to extending the life of other association assets

9. Reserve funding

Most reserve professionals will tell you that your reserve fund should be "off limits" as a way for an association find their way out a deep financial problem. But, future funds will do you no good if you can not survive. The original assumptions for building a reserve funding plan may or may not still apply. A responsible BoD experiencing a tough economic time must examine every area of cost reduction opportunity, including the reserve funding strategy. It may very well find that it can find a more optimum balance between meeting current and future needs.

10. Taxes

Certiorari, or the act of challenging property's annual real estate tax assessment, is among the least understood ways in which an association can keep it costs down. The basis of certiorari filing is the fact that the taxing unit often makes mistakes in property valuations. Left unchallenged, these mistakes can go on forever, resulting in the overpayment of real estate taxes for as long as the building stands.

Appendix F – Standard Format for Displaying Cost-Savings Information

ABC Condominium Association

Cost Reduction Area - Insert Title Here

Background:

(Briefly summarize the cost reduction area possibility and background information. This is similar to an executive summary, where the reader can get a quick grasp of the issue being considered, without reading volumes of information.)

Data and Pertinent Information:

(List the key facts here that the decision makers should take into account. This should be in summary form and should only contain the most pertinent information. You do not have to have agreement on the information and there may be differing viewpoints. The underlying assumption is that if reasonable people have the same information, then it can be reasonably expected that they will come to the same conclusion)

Recommendations/Alternatives to Be Considered:

(This section should contain any viable alternative course of action that could be taken. It is a brainstorming list of possibilities. Often, one or more alternatives can be combined into a stronger new alternative. Eventually, the Team Leader (or other person making the recommendation) will have to decide what s/he will recommend. An easy way to state that recommendation is to answer the question, "If I were the Board of Directors, what decision would I make? This recommendation should be described in sufficient detail that it can stand on its own.)

Appendix G – Arrears Payment Collection

Background:

The smooth and ongoing financial operation of any homeowner or condo association depends almost exclusively on the timely and complete payment by unit owners of their monthly maintenance/common charges. Failure to meet this obligation on the parts of only a few can lead to an association's failure to meet its own obligations and to force it to raise fees on the remaining members. This in turn can cause yet further delinquencies or default payments. Coupled with rising interest rates and falling property values, this vicious cycle continues as more homeowners strain to make their monthly mortgage payment. Those now wishing to sell or refinance their property are met with decreased property values and higher maintenance fees making it more difficult and unattractive to prospective buyers. An association BoD should react very quickly and firmly to any payments in arrears to prevent this "death spiral" from occurring.

Data and Pertinent Information:

- Each state has a collection process in its laws and you should become very familiar with them before embarking upon any collection action to be taken.
- The collection of unpaid assessments is one of the most important responsibilities of a BoD. Whether they realize it or not, all associations adopt a collection policy. Some do it unintentionally and without realizing what they have adopted; others deliberate and consciously adopt a policy that fits their needs.
- For some financially distressed homeowners, paying association dues is often a low priority, People are generally not going to miss their utility payment because they don't want that to get turned off and sometimes

association fees move down on the priority ladder, particularly if collection procedures are weak or lax.

- It's important to act quickly if and when a unit owner defaults. A typical problem for associations is when they don't move fast enough, sometimes because of sympathy. Collecting delinquent assessments from any owner becomes almost exponentially harder with the accumulation of every additional delinquent assessment, so the earlier that the association begins collecting, the better.

- It is absolutely imperative that association members understand their financial obligation and the consequences for not paying in a timely fashion. A clearly worded, communicated and enforced collection policy is the solution to collections, since the course of action is predetermined. By having a written collection policy, it simplifies one of the Board's most disagreeable tasks: collecting money from neighbors.

- A well-drafted collection policy provides a road map and checklist to guide the Board in handling delinquencies. It clearly sets forth a step by step process and specifies each individual's role. It also provides a mechanism to exercise discretion where unforeseen circumstances such as loss of employment, illness, or death of a wage earner, call for compassion in negotiating a payment arrangement. Where it is clear in advance what is to be done, by whom and when, there is no time or effort wasted in trying to figure out what to do next. Adhering to the specified procedure in every instance of homeowner delinquency ensures the consistent, non-discriminatory and, predictable handling of collecting assessments.

- All communication to delinquent owners should be in writing. This will help to eliminate communication problems and will be necessary to produce if you end up in court. Be sure to keep copies of all correspondence that you issue.

- There are only two reasons why co-owners fail to pay what they owe: they will not pay or they cannot pay. "Willnots" are scarce; "Cannots" are becoming more numerous. Publishing the name of a "will not" is apt to increase animosity, not lessen it. Publishing the names of "Cannots" will do nothing to solve the underlying inability to pay. Publishing names of delinquents could lead to lawsuits for libel, false light and/or intentional infliction of emotional distress.

- During depressed economic times, a BoD should anticipate an increase in the number of owners who are delinquent in payment of association assessments and should plan ahead on how they will address the expected rise in unpaid assessments. This is particularly true when bankruptcies are involved and banks are unwilling to pay association dues or conform to certain CCR's

- In simpler times, homeowners associations had a powerful enforcement tool at hand: the lien. An indebted homeowner who wanted to sell or refinance would have to first clear the lien. But a foreclosure wipes away an association lien, meaning a lawsuit is often the only way to collect back payments. Some of the debtors are investors who have little equity in the homes and are willing to walk away from a bad investment.

- Most mortgage documents let the lender consider a mortgage loan in default as soon as monthly assessment charges are in arrears, even if the mortgage itself is still being paid on time. This puts additional pressure on the owner to sell or pay their fees.

- "Upside Down" is a term used to describe owners who owe more on their property than the property is worth. This happens during down-turns in the economy and causes many homeowners to walk away from their properties or declare bankruptcy. If the owner "walks away" from the property, he/she continues to live in the property but stops paying the lender (and stops paying the association as well). Both the bank and the association generally initiate foreclosure proceedings against the owner. However, banks are often slow to foreclose because they don't want the property in their inventory. As a result, the association ursue its own collection efforts without counting on the bank. Also, Boards should consider budgeting for bad debt.

- The practice of "Buy and Bail" is where the home buyer purchases (the "buy"), for example, a more affordable dwelling with the intention to cease making payments on the previous home's mortgage (the "bail"). Among the various reasons for a home buyer to engage in this practice may be they owe the bank more money than the house is worth, they could no longer afford their monthly mortgage payments, or they simply have found a more affordable or nicer home and can't sell the home they are vacating. But how can homeowners get a loan for a new home if they are barely able to make their current payments? In many cases, they tell the underwriters they plan to rent out the first house and seek to use that income to qualify for a new mortgage on their new principal residence. In essence, they are trying to qualify and secure the mortgage on the new home before the severely negative consequences the "pending" foreclosure on the first home will have on their credit rating. While the "buy and bail" solution may seem like a good idea to some, there are repercussions for the homeowner, their communities, and real estate professionals.

- As of May 1, 2008, Fannie Mae and Freddie Mac (the entities that buy most home mortgage loans) responded to the mounting loan delinquencies and defaults by revising their underwriting guidelines for financing residential mortgages. Changes include:
  - The homeowner association has an "adequate" budget.
  - The budget allocates at least 10% of annual revenues to reserves.
  - The HOA holds funds equaling the deductible under the master insurance policy.
  - No more than 15% of the common area fees are delinquent by more than one month.

- All of these changes are significant for lenders, but the delinquency limit is likely to prove most problematic. Even with an aggressive collection policy in place, it takes time to collect delinquent payments or to foreclose on delinquent owners.

- It is not uncommon for lenders to lose over $50,000 per home sold in foreclosure; therefore, associations should expect to write off some assessment debt as uncollectible.

- Although it will be denied, a practice among banks and lending institutions is to not foreclose on a property for months or years to avoid paying association fees. This is particularly true if there are state laws that require some type of penalty payment to the association when the property is foreclosed. Banks argue that they have no way of knowing when homeowners stop paying association fees and assessments. It is not until after 90 days of nonpayment on the mortgage that banks have any right to file a notice of default. Nine months typically elapse from the day that the homeowner stops paying until the day that the bank owns the home again and during that time banks have no rights relative to the property. Association members are frustrated because some of the foreclosed homes become eyesores before/during/after the whole foreclosure process.

- Key findings of the 2008 Florida Community Association Mortgage Foreclosure Survey of 500 communities last spring:
    - Almost 60 percent reported that mortgage lenders who have foreclosed on units or homes are not currently paying monthly maintenance fees and/or other assessments as required by law.
    - Four out of every 10 respondents reported units or home left vacant for six months or more. One in five said units have been uninhabited for a year or more.
    - 66 percent said their associations intend to increase maintenance fees or special assessments to compensate for anticipated shortfalls due to declining collections from foreclosures.

- When it comes to getting banks to follow homeowners association regulations on foreclosed homes, the key is to fine them heavily to get their attention and for them to stop the financial liability clock from ticking on them.

Recommendations/Alternatives to Be Considered:

- If the condominium or homeowner association does not yet have a written late-fee and collection policy, this should be its highest priority. Define every step in the process, timing requirements, and individual responsibilities. The process should automatically happen no matter what. By publishing and distributing this policy to all owners, there is no confusion. It is no longer personal but just the process by which fees are collected. Collection policies should conform to state statutes and the governing documents, clearly written, reasonable, and universally applied. See *Appendix H* for a sample policy. You can also do an Internet search on condo or homeowner association delinquent policy for more examples. Show below is a general approach and some considerations when developing such a policy.
  - Review the association governing documents and applicable statutes to determine the remedies for collection of assessments, such as liens or court suit.
  - Implement the available remedies by adopting a collection policy which clearly states the procedures to be followed to collect delinquent assessments. Charge unit owners substantially for late condo fee payments and provide for graduated sanctions.
  - Notify owners of the association collection policy, including applicable late fees, interest and collection costs which delinquent owners will incur. Communicate the collection process regularly and through different types of media, to assure that all association members completely understand the policy and its implications to them

- Amend the association governing documents, where needed, to provide for late fees, interest, collection costs and attorney fees to be assessed against delinquent owners and to permit acceleration of payment of assessments.

- Maintain clear and complete owner account records showing all charges and payments. This will be necessary documentation if collection actions are required. Also, many real estate firms and/or prospective purchasers of pre-owned condominiums request an up-to-date estoppel certificate before considering the purchase of a particular unit. This certificate is often seen as equivalent to the disclosure statement required in the sale of new condominiums. It contains information in respect of the common expense obligations of the owner and of default in payment, if any, together with statements and information as prescribed by the regulations.

- Take prompt collection action against delinquent owners.

  - If the collection procedures have been lax in your association, give everyone a 30-day "grace period" to bring themselves up-to-date. Let them know that after that, they'll not only be paying what owe in back assessments, but a very expensive legal bill also, possibly liens and foreclosures. If someone has a legitimate hardship case let them make their case to the BoD and then decide if you want to work them on a structured re-payment program.

  - If the delinquency seems likely to be short-lived, a compromise is often more effective. Sit down with the owner and try to set up a payment plan, but be ready to quickly reinstate stronger action if the resident fails to meet these scaled-down commitments. Associations also can offer payment plans or loans, or waive late fees or penalties to help owners to catch up on delinquent dues. Shown below is an example of an amnesty program intended to cut down on legal fees and collect past due fees:

- For one year, the Association will do partial to complete waiver of late fees if unit owners who are delinquent with their assessments bring them current within 12 months. This program will only apply to unit owners who (1) haven't been referred to the Association attorney and (2) haven't had a collection against them during the last 24 months. If the unit owners become current with ALL fees within 12 months, the Association will waive 50% of the late fees, 75% if brought current within six months and 100% if brought current within 90 days. Unit owners must agree to an automatic deduction from their bank account and must be paid by the 15th of the month (our fees are due on the 1st and considered late if paid after the 15th) If the deduction does not go through even once, the agreement will be cancelled.

— Rely on the professionals (accountants, lawyers, managers and collection agencies) for advice. As a volunteer, recognize the limits of your expertise. Apart from encouraging the members of your entire association to pay assessments, avoid unduly pressuring anyone into paying dues. Refrain from discussing other owners' financial problems outside of Board meetings.

— File a lien. A board's most potent weapon is a lien, filed against a delinquent property. A lien is a legal claim that ensures payment of a debt from any profit when a property is sold. If your Board can't collect association fees, don't let the situation drag on; file a lien as quickly as the law and your collection policy allow. It's important to get the association's claim on record, even though the bank has priority in collecting payment if the home is sold. In a foreclosure, properties are often worth less than the mortgage so there's nothing for the associations to collect. In any case, a lien serves another purpose: It signals to a homeowner that the Board is serious about collection and may inspire some owners to pay their delinquent fees. Recording the lien creates a public record of debt, and serves as a reminder of the debt to title companies who are preparing for closings. A lean is the final non-legal request for the property owner to become current in payment of his/her assessments.

– Make wider use of collection agencies. Most of these agencies work on a contingent fee basis, whereby they only get paid if they collect. That may sound attractive until you consider that the net result to the association will *never* be payment in full. Governing documents typically allow associations to recover their actual reasonable attorney fees in collection matters, but makes no specific provision for recovering contingent fees imposed by collection agencies. Some collection agencies will only pursue collection if there is no mortgage foreclosure and no bankruptcy involved.

– Go to court. When you simply cannot collect a unit's fees, you can take a property owner to court -- usually small claims court. Where the amount of the delinquency is small, it may be advisable to sue for a money judgment rather than commencing a judicial foreclosure. Money judgments may be particularly attractive where an owner is employed. In this instance, the owner's wages or bank account can often be garnished relatively quickly and inexpensively to collect on the judgment. Garnishment involves the issuance of a court order after a judgment, which requires a bank, employer, or other creditor of the defendant, to withhold and turn over to the court any money in its possession. Where a bank or other lender with a senior lien has foreclosed on the unit, the only option open to the association will be a personal judgment against the prior owner for money due. Condo or homeowner association delinquencies don't show up on an owner's credit record, but failing to pay a court-ordered debt does. When investors are involved, getting a judgment from the courts may allow the association to "reach and apply" towards the delinquent dues any rents the owner is getting from tenants in those units.

- Your governing documents may stipulate that association amenities and recreation facilities can be denied for those in arrears for such things as; snow removal, trash pick-up, grass mowing, landscaping, pool, tennis courts, reserved parking, access to visitor parking., suspend gate access cards, and even voting)? As long as they are receiving the same services as those who ARE paying, there may be little incentive for them to ever pay up and you may have to wait until they sell their unit to collect through the filed lien. If this stipulation is not in the governing documents they you might want to consider modifying them.
- Address Foreclosures and Delinquencies.
  - Increase the fine amount for not maintaining property, especially for covenant violations by lender owners. Increase the kinds of violations that could result in fines. Fine for specific situations rather than general circumstances. For example, don't just have a fine for landscaping, but have a fine for a dead tree, for weeds, for dead plants, for the sprinkler system. Each one should be a fineable issue. Pile on the fines and when the banks starting receiving invoices for $500 a week for each home in violation, they will start to pay attention. To use this strategy, you will have to know the CC&Rs (conditions, covenants and deed restrictions) inside and out, and if they're not strong, look at ways to modify them.
  - Take advantage of blight laws that some cities have adopted.
  - Speed up the collection process, especially for delinquent lender owners.
  - Sell bad debt to a third party. When there is equity in the property, there may be a third party investor who is interested in purchasing the association's lien. As the owner of the lien, the association is free to assign or sell that lien to any third party. Investors are

attracted to association liens because liens provide them with the opportunity to redeem or purchase a property in foreclosure, usually at a discounted rate in comparison to the property's fair market value. By selling its lien to an interested investor, the association can usually recover for the full amount due, including all unpaid assessments, fees, and attorney fees and costs due on the account. If a property has a large amount of equity in it, the association's lien can often be assigned for more than what is even owed on the account. Another benefit to the association is that investors are much more likely to protect and preserve the property, make necessary repairs, and prepare the house for resale than to sell banks, which often let their properties sit in disrepair until resale. Assigning the association's lien is done at no cost and with no liability to the association. A contract for assignment of the association's lien should be prepared by the association's attorney and should state the investor is merely purchasing the lien, and is not receiving any representation or guarantee that he or she will end up owning the property through the foreclosure. The cost of preparing this document should be added to the price of the lien and paid for by the investor.

– An association may want to foreclose quickly, before the lender does. An association lien is inferior to a claim brought by a lender holding the mortgage. So if a bank files first, the association may not be able to collect the back dues.

– If foreclosures are involved and the banks are unwilling to pay fees or conform to certain CCR's, be consistent in the enforcement practices with them, even though there is little likelihood that it will produce the intended results. It will help prevent animosity with the remaining owners.

– During this recent rash of foreclosures, some condo attorneys are generally recommending that associations sue unit owners in Civil

Court for money judgments, rather than going the foreclosure route. This often is much faster and less expensive and can still result in an auction sale of the unit. It also provides the association with access to other assets such as bank accounts and wages to satisfy the common charges arrears once a judgment is entered. They further recommend that lawsuits for money judgments be filed with the Small Claims Part of the Civil Court. While the amount of the recovery is limited by the jurisdictional limit of the Small Claims Part (i.e. $5,000), it is much quicker and less expensive than regular Civil Court. Rather than litigating for months or years, your attorney can literally spend a few hours in court at a hearing where a repayment agreement with the delinquent unit owner can often be negotiated.

- A little known, but attractive, method to collect common charge arrears is available in some states where a unit owner rents their unit to a tenant. In those situations, the law authorizes associations to collect rent payments directly from the tenants of unit owners in arrears. This is accomplished by sending a notice to the tenants pursuant to the statute. When the statute does not provide the condominium association with any legal remedy against the tenant if he or she disregards the notice it can be remedied by putting language in an association's lease application, which authorizes the association to sue a unit owner's tenant directly.

- Budget for bad debt. Associations typically build a small percentage for delinquencies into their budgets as a safeguard. Today, more and more Boards are increasing the amount from 2% to 10%, depending on the size of the property. When speculators comprise a large proportion of owners, you'll want to generously pad your budget. Consult with the association's attorney and accountant as to when and how to write off uncollectible assessments and related charges.

- Get outside help for your accounts receivables. If your BoD does not have the interest, desire, time, or expertise to go after delinquent accounts, another option is to use an outside company that specializes in this type of activity. Companies such as, Association Financial Services, which are backed by private investors, gives associations a cash advance to cover its shortfall and use for maintenance, landscaping, repairs and other association responsibilities. In exchange, it takes over associations' accounts receivables, billing members for their regular payments and attempts to collect past-due payments. The company makes money by charging a monthly service fee that usually ranges less than $10 per unit. It also charges a fee matching the amount of late fees and interest on past-due fees. Claims by these companies are that they are able to reduce delinquencies by collecting on past assessments more efficiently than the associations themselves. The use of any such companies should be reviewed with the association attorney to assure that there are no legal concerns.

- Be smart! You do not want to invest heavily in attorney fees, filing fees, or court costs if you do not have a more than reasonable expectation of ever collecting your past due money. And, the money that you expect to collect should be more than what you spend. You will have to use good judgment. You can continue to put liens even if you don't decide to foreclose. If you find you are spending more money then it brings in, then find a cheaper way to file the lien. In some states, it is a simple process that does not require the services of an attorney and can be filed for as little as $50. While a lien won't get your money in most foreclosures, it will get your money in a short sale. The only method of causing you to lose money when a lien is filed is if a higher lien forecloses. Then the liens are settled in order of priority. The government always gets its money. Then the first mortgage and after that the association.

- Another consideration is that the association will lose if significant costs associated with a lean or attorney costs forces someone in arrears into foreclosure. In that case, it is in the best interest of the association try to work with the owner who request help, but also be ready to follow through with your normal collection procedures for those who won't work you or fail to keep up their end of the agreement.

Appendix H – Sample Fee & Assessment Collection Policy

The ABC Condominium Association
Fee & Assessment Collection Policy

Condo fees and assessments are the financial lifeblood of the association as they are the association's primary source of income. Therefore, the Board of Directors with use the following policy, when collecting fees and assessments:

A) Collection policies should conform to state statutes and the governing documents, clearly written, reasonable, and universally applied.

B) Communicate the collection process regularly and through different types of media, to assure that all association members completely understand the policy and its implications to them

C) Provide for graduated sanctions for untimely payments.

D) Do not make exceptions as this money belongs to all of the co-owners and they have a right to expect that it is collected in a timely fashion

E) Treat co-owners with respect and dignity throughout the collection process. Make every effort to resolve delinquencies directly with the co-owner and without third party intervention

The ABC Condominium Association
Fee & Assessment Collection Process

TIMING	ACTION
10 days prior to the due date	Association Treasurer will send out notification of condo fee payment due date
First day of the quarter (January, April, July, October)	Condo fees are due
10 calendar days after due date	A reminder letter/email will be sent out
30 calendar days after due date	A default late payment charge of $50 will be applied and interest will accrue at a per annum rate of 10% from the initial due date until the fee has been paid. A letter/email will be sent

	describing the amount that is owed along with a written description of this collection process and the applicable by-laws.
45 calendar days after due date	A communication letter/email will be sent out describing additional collection steps that will be taken if fees are not paid
60 calendar days after due date	Account will be turned over to a collection agency or attorney for further action, which could include a suit, lien and/or property foreclosure. A delinquent unit owner will be responsible for attorneys' fees and costs incurred in collecting delinquent charges, per condo association governing documents.
Special Circumstances	All co-owners should be aware that if they are having a difficult time paying their condo fee, due to serious illness, unemployment, etc., we will try to work out a payment schedule with them.

- Additional clarification is provided below for the highlighted area:

Collection Enforcement Mechanics	Resp.
1) **Special Circumstances** - If the co-owner is unable to meet the fee/assessment obligations in a timely manner, due to circumstances beyond their control (loss of job, sickness, death, family emergency, acts of god, etc.), a request for special treatment may be made to the Board within sixty (60) days of the initial delinquency or it will be considered waived. Where discretion is authorized, the BoD should ensure that decisions are based upon well-understood and uniformly-applied principles, and are made in a fair and non-discriminatory manner. While the immediate payment of all sums due is the most desirable settlement result, this may not always be possible. To ensure that the co-owner will be able to pay the sums due, settlements may call for payments over a period of time. A	Co-Owner

	contract agreement should be prepared which specifies an exact amount that an owner must pay by a specific date that is agreed upon and signed by both parties.	
2)	**Lien Recording** - Where the Board's attempts to resolve the delinquency through written communication are unsuccessful after 60 calendar days, a lien will be placed on the Unit. The recording of a lien against the condominium unit is the most important action the association can take. It secures payment of the delinquent assessments and acts as a "red flag" for the delinquent owner. It is the final non-legal request for the co-owner to become current in payment of his/her assessments. The association Secretary will provide their attorney the following information: a) Unit number b) Copy of the owner's deed c) Mailing address for owner of record (particularly if a non occupant owner) d) Tax identification number for the unit e) A clear unit ledger reflecting assessments, late charges and legal cost separately and identifying any payments maid by the owner as well as the current balance. Once prepared, the lien must be timely recorded with the county register of deeds and served on the co-owner.	Pres./ Sec'y
3)	**Turn Over To Legal Council For Collection** - If the lien is not paid off in a timely manner the association lawyer will be advised to proceed with collection procedures. Once an account is turned over, all further communications between the association and the debtor are to be handled directly between the association's attorney and the owner, or the owner's attorney. Owners attempting to appeal directly to the Board will be advised to work it out with the Association's attorney. The association Secretary will provide their attorney the following information: a) the name of the association and the name and phone number of its contact person; b) the address to be used for communications regarding the account; c) the billing address for the association, if it is different; d) the owner's name, the owner's address or mailing address, if different; e) the owner's telephone numbers; f) the name and telephone numbers of any tenants if the premises is not owner occupied; g) any information which the association has collected with	Pres./ Sec'y

regard to the owner's bank accounts; h) descriptions and license numbers of the owner's vehicles; i) the name, address, and loan number of the mortgage lender on the unit; j) a copy of the declarations of covenants, conditions and restrictions, bylaws, articles of incorporation and the association's collection policy; k) a ledger for the account showing all debits and credits from the time that the delinquent account was last current to the present time; l) a copy of any association lien which has been recorded; m) all correspondence relating to the delinquency or which might relate to a claim or defense by the owner against the association; n) all documents received by the association regarding a foreclosure against the owner or a bankruptcy by the owner; o) if a special assessment is involved, a copy of the resolution approving the special assessment which encompasses the amounts and due dates of the assessment.	
4) **Begin Collection Proceedings** - the attorney will probably send a demand letter to the co-owner to inform him/her of the amount that is owed and that legal action may ensue if the amount is not paid. If there is no response to the demand letter, the next step is to commence a lawsuit against the co-owner for the assessments owed to the association. Often several courses of action are available to the association. The association usually has the option to sue the owner personally for money judgment or foreclose the association's lien for assessments resulting in a judicial foreclosure. It is the role of the attorney, in consideration with the Board, to consider the facts and circumstances of each case and recommend an appropriate strategy for proceeding that may include the following: a) **Money Judgment** - Where the amount of the delinquency is small, it will usually be advisable to sue for a money judgment rather than commencing a judicial foreclosure. Money judgments may be particularly attractive where an owner is employed. In this instance, the owner's wages or bank account can often be garnished relatively quickly and inexpensively to collect on the judgment. Garnishment involves the issuance of a court order after a judgment, which requires a bank, employer, or other creditor of the defendant, to withhold	**Board/ Atty.**

and turn over to the court, for the benefit of the association, any money in its possession. Where a bank or other lender with a senior lien has foreclosed on the unit, the only option open to the association will be a personal judgment against the prior owner for money due.

b) **Payment Agreement** – In some instances to ensure that the owner(s) will be able to pay the sums due, settlements may call for payments over a period of time. A stipulation for judgment or payment agreement should be used to document any settlement agreement and installment payment plan. A stipulation for judgment is a document signed by the owner which, unlike a normal contract, may provide the basis for entry of a judgment against the debtor without a trial. A stipulation specifies an exact amount that an owner must pay by a specific date that is agreed upon by both parties. Thus, if the owner does not comply with the stipulation requirements, the association can automatically enter judgment against the owner. After judgment is entered, the association may garnish the co-owners wages and bank accounts.

c) **Foreclosure of the condominium lien.** - The Board will do whatever they can to avoid foreclosing. Not only can it become a highly emotional situation, it also can become an expensive problem that takes months or even years to work through. For all parties involved, finding an alternative is almost always preferable to foreclosure. However, foreclosure may be the recommended option where a co-owner has had repeated delinquencies, if the amount of the assessment obligation is over $1,000.00, and if the owner's equity in the unit is substantial. Foreclosure may also be the preferred alternative if an owner lives out of the state or country and the association wants to limit its costs and enhance its chances of collecting the delinquent amount. Finally, foreclosure may be the only remedy available to the association if an owner has no other assets or income, or has gone through a bankruptcy

Appendix I – Management Company Services

Background:

One of the primary duties of a Board of Directors (BoD) is to manage the affairs of the association. Depending upon BoD member's level of expertise, time, and interest, it may choose to delegate some of the management functions. Following are the three forms of management typically found in associations:

1) **Self-Management.** With this type of management the BoD directly manages the association, often using committees to assist in the management.

2) **Management Company.** Some associations will employ the services of a professional Management Company to handle management functions. This can include assessment collection, property inspections, soliciting bids for Board review, correspondence, meeting attendance, etc.

3) **Association Employed/Onsite Management**. Some large associations choose to hire a professional manager to work on-site, as an employee of the association.

The reasons for an association using a Management Company can range from "convenience" for some to a "necessity" for others. But, if an association's BoD is facing a severe financial condition, it may have to take on more of these direct management duties than it would prefer. Since the use of a Management Company can represent a major expense to an association (some are upwards of 30% of the annual budget), it is an area of cost reduction opportunity that cannot be ignored.

There are several things that should be highlighted regarding the use a Management Company.

- While management companies can simplify things for a condo or homeowner association BoD, they do not replace the BoD. A Management Company reports to and receives its direction from the BoD and not the other way around. The BoD has hiring/firing authority and can eliminate, replace, revise, or renegotiate a contract with a Management Company.

- Inexperienced BoD's must guard against a Management Company "dependency" where the Management Company is calling all the shots and the BoD is merely a rubber stamp. A good Management Company can be a real benefit to your company. They do bring experience, an extra set of hands, and usually ideas tried and proven in a condo or homeowner association environment. Likewise, a good Management Company should always attempt to impart their management skills to inexperienced BoD members. A good BoD will insist that this is the way that they want to operate with a Management Company. Inexperienced BoD members may want to consider a "shadow consulting" relationship when it comes to management and leadership issues. The idea is for the Management Company to remain behind the scenes, advising and training the inexperienced BoD members. This ensures that the BoD is seen as the leader of the association. The goal of shadow consulting is to transfer the skills and experiences to the BoD, thus increasing the likelihood of effective management and long-term solutions.

- A BoD has a fiduciary responsibility to the association for which it serves. This fiduciary relationship requires the members of the BoD to act in good faith and in the best interests of the members of the association and that they exercise due care and diligence. A fiduciary obligation represents the highest level of responsibility under the law. Unlike a Contractor, a Management Company acts as an **agent** of the association and is also held to the same fiduciary responsibility as the BoD. Likewise, it has a duty to manage association's costs in the most effective way possible.

- A Management Company, like any company, is only as good as its people. They may not have the necessary skill sets to attack cost reductions and may have "blind spots" that prevent them from examining new ways to attack cost creep that will eventually come into play. Like the BoD, they too can also fall into the complacency trap of simply meeting cost increases by raising association fees. Today's Management Company must do more than review monthly budget reports, handle violation notices, or perform the daily maintenance activities. They must minimize costs at every opportunity and come up with creative ways for condo and homeowner associations to combat rising costs or economic downturns.

- The relationship between an association BoD and its Management Company is usually a deep one, and one that can last for a long time. The longer a working relationship lasts, the better the two parties understand one another and work together. But, it also may be more difficult for an association BoD to change suppliers or to address a lackadaisical cost reduction performance. A responsible BoD must take any action that is necessary and to set the expectation with its Management Company that cost reduction is one of its primary responsibilities. It is also their job to replace them if they are unable to deliver.

If an association BoD chooses to use a particular Management Company, it should expect a relentless effort to help them reduce their costs. This is a new concept for many, as they are much more comfortable with just delivering the services outlined in the contract. Take a look at your existing contract or a proposal from a potential Management Company. Do you see a statement that says they will deliver cost savings to the association? Or better yet, do you see a statement that says they will deliver (X)% of cost savings to the association?   A Management Company like any other supplier does not like to be pinned down. It often easier to just deliver the service and pass alone any cost increases to association members in the form of increased fees or special assessments. Management Companies should be held accountable for cost performance and a provision should be incorporated into their contract to reinforce that responsibility.

Data and Pertinent Information:

- The cost for professional management can vary greatly depending on several variables including:
    - The number of Units and location
    - The services desired, including: number of meetings and number of inspections; number of contractors; amount and content of common areas; and the number of amenities
    - The Management Company's expenses, desired profit margin, and competitor's rates
    - The salary levels of the Management Company staff can also have a major impact on the management fees. If an association BoD wants experienced professionals, there is a hefty price to pay.
- Professional management is (in most instances) pure overhead cost. Although some overhead is needed, it contributes very little, if anything, to the direct quality of life in a small to mid-size, well-functioning association.
- Regardless of the number of members, professional management may be necessary under the following conditions:
    - In associations with a clubhouse, swimming pool or other such amenities.
    - Associations that have sizeable budgets or legal exposure.

- In a development that has a large number of absentee or part-time resident owners

- There is no doubt that a good Management Company can come into an association and find cost savings opportunities. They often claim that they can pay for their services from the savings that are generated. However, there are two important factors that should be considered with this argument:
    - This same service could be provided by an outside consultant who could assess the site and operation of the association and make recommendations on how to reduce costs. The benefit here is that a consultant represents a one-time cost, while a Management Company is a re-occurring cost.
    - If the association employs a new Management Company who generates savings to offset their costs, the association as a whole is no better off – it is a wash. If the association implemented the costs saving improvements itself, then it would be a savings to the association.

- One of the major reasons that associations hire a Management Company is that they do not have the required expertise to run their association's business. After all, they are volunteers. If this lack of expertise exists, then they may also have problems with holding the Management Company accountable or establishing cost reduction expectations with them.

- Not all self-managed communities depend exclusively on volunteers. Some hire individual employees or contract with one or more firms to perform maintenance or administrative chores when the association does not have the time or expertise.

- If you use a Management Company, an area that deserves close scrutiny for cost reduction is any routine services that may be provided. This includes such things as routine maintenance, security guards, office help, etc. What is the hourly charge for the services being provided? How does this compare for the local going rate for private contractors or apartment buildings? Do not let your Management Company bully you on this one by saying that it is not possible to directly hire someone to provide these services. It is possible and often advisable. This can be an area for a Management Company to get "healthy" at your expense, by charging you a high prevailing rate and paying the person at a much lower rate (i.e. – profit for them). If you use this strategy, there are a couple of considerations that you should be made aware of:

- If you hire a person as an employee to perform this function, under the law, you are required to pay payroll taxes, benefits, and workers compensation insurance. You also have the added administrative responsibility of keeping payroll records, generating payment checks, and filing income tax statements. A way to avoid this unpleasant administrative task is to have the payroll administered thru a payroll company (like ADP or Paychex). They will deal with the taxes, benefits, and insurance. All you will have to do is fax in 'timesheets' to the company and they prepare the payroll. You will get detailed information on your costs and thru electronic funds transfer, you can pay the company.

- Some associations only use independent contractors as a way to avoid payroll taxes, health benefits, and workers compensation insurance. To avoid misclassification of employees in the eyes of the government, associations should limit the use of "full-time" independent contractors, and instead hire workers on a specific project basis. Additionally, associations should treat workers similarly in similar situations. In other words, if the job duties of two employees are the same or similar, do not hire one as an independent contractor and the other as an employee.

- A Management Company sells its time and the more time spent on your homeowner association business, the greater the cost. One of the big time consumers is preparing for and following up on BoD meetings. Managers spend sometimes as much as 80% their time gathering information, preparing management reports, reviewing the financial statement, communicating relevant information, putting decision packages together, and other administrative functions.

- While staff salaries are fixed, there are ways to lower the cost of employee salaries. Overtime pay, at time-and-a-half, can be a serious burden on an association's budget. It is therefore crucial to keep overtime expenses to a minimum. Nevertheless, many BoD's consider overtime pay an unavoidable expense and spend a significant portion of their budgets on this cost, when it should only be an occasional expense.

Re*commendations/Alternatives to Be Considered:*

- Determine the level of self-management that you will use and that you can afford.
    - Take apart the Management Company contract line-item-by-line item and explore alternative ways to eliminate, revise it, or have the service performed by someone else at a lower cost.
    - Separate the association "needs" from its "wants"
    - Have the Management Company provide quotes for each line item in the contract. This will allow for an apples-to-apples comparison with self management or other suppliers.
    - Use this eliminated or reduced service level as a basis to renegotiate a lower priced contract.
    - Use consultants, freelances or part-time employees, instead of full-time employees.

– Often, one of the largest expenses is bookkeeping. If you have an active volunteer group that is willing to take over some management tasks, you can realize significant savings by hiring an accountant to handle the books and to process payments/receipts.

- **Competitively source your small service projects.** For small service needs, it is not necessary to have a Management Company or professional contractor perform small maintenance tasks or to fix every little problem.

  – **Handyman Services.** For condo or homeowner associations that can't afford a full time maintenance person, contract with a licensed, bonded and insured handyman who can perform a monthly "laundry list" of small repairs. Combine tasks to provide a full day's work.

  – **Apartment Service Providers.** Another way to determine if you are getting the "best deal" from your Management Company when it comes to routing maintenance services is to contact companies who provide this type of property maintenance for apartment complexes.

  – **Moonlighters.** In most buildings, the building staff moonlights as painters and general repairpersons. Talk to your staff and see if they would like to make extra money by doing some of the work that normally a professional would do. The best example of this approach is touch-up painting in halls and stairwells. Develop a closer alliance with subcontractors to perform work in the neighborhood to get small projects done quickly and cost effectively.

  – **Volunteers.** You may have members who have special skills/hobbies (engineers, contractors, woodworkers, gardeners, skilled trades, etc.) who may be willing to perform small maintenance duties or projects. Do no be afraid to ask for their help. The use of volunteers is an excellent way to help keep your costs down.

- Jointly explore with the Management Company any changes that the association cold make to reduce the Management Company cost that in turn could be passed along to the association.
  - Eliminate or reduce the amount of time that a Management Company is required at BoD meetings.
    - Shorten the length of BoD meetings. Hold quarterly meetings versus monthly meetings
    - Hold daytime meetings during normal business hours to avoid overtime
    - Move the Board meeting to the management office to save manager time and avoid mileage charges
    - With an approved budget, proper policies in place and a management planning calendar, the Management Company should be able to handle most issues with only occasional input from the president.
  - Reconfigure how a Management Company handles administration of insurance claims and damage reconstruction. Insurance matters can take many hours of a Management Company's time. If the contract agreement specifically states that insurance claim work is an extra cost to the association, the Management Company can bill the insurance claim for the time it takes to administrate a claim and renovation work. A similar principle involves time spent on collections or legal action against an owner. This management time should be billed to the delinquent owner.
  - Rather than having the association bear the cost for preparing sale disclosure statements to owners who are selling their homes and buyers' lenders, have the Management Company bill owners and buyers separately for this service.
  - Scale back on the frequency of services that are offered.
    - Limited office hours or lengthened response time
    - Offer part-time services for security, gate/door attendance

- Send out association dues on a quarterly basis versus a monthly basis. Allow members to pay dues on a semi-annual or annual basis, if desired.
- Hold minor repair items until enough are accumulated to allow for a more efficient utilization of maintenance contractor's time
- Conduct less frequent inspections for CC&R violations and batch process related notices.
- Use electronic communications to members and record keeping to eliminate paper, filing, stamps, mail handling, etc. Allow for electronic payment of association fees.
- Eliminate all overtime and transportation expenses for Management Company employees

- Include in the Management Company contract a specific reference to the expected level of cost savings efforts required of the Management Company. This could be in the form of a specific amount or a percentage of operating costs. Then, conduct a performance review with the Management Company on the progress being/not being made. It is not uncommon for companies to demand a 10-15% annual cost savings from their internal departments or outside suppliers.
- A more aggressive approach to reducing a Management Company costs is to negotiate a yearly reduction in fees (i.e. – 3% - 5%) that it charges an association, due to its cost savings efforts and learning curve experiences as it becomes familiar with association operations.
- Go out and get competitive bids and bring them back to your current Management Company so they have the opportunity to lower their price for you. Large service contracts like a Management Company should be competitively bid every year or two. Even if you are totally satisfied with the service received and have no intention of changing providers, it will demonstrate to the membership that the BoD is practicing due diligence and good stewardship. Also, if a particular Management

Company is maneuvering for a contract increase, a competitive proposal will work to the association's advantage in negotiating or verifying that the current Management Company is entirely justified in the increase. If it is to the advantage of the association, negotiate a long-term contract with the Management Company that states in exchange for a competitive price, the association will not seek competing competitive bids for a certain period of time.

- Confront your Management Company if it announces a price increase and re-bid the order where appropriate.

- Explore "partnering" with other associations to award combined contracts to the most competitive Management Company quote.

- Request that your Management Company prepare recommendations on ways for the association to reduce association waste, increase efficiency, or save money.

- Develop a scorecard for keeping track of Management Company service, quality, delivery and pricing. Implement a monitoring program (metrics, customer complaint system) to better understand the service / issues.

- Install a performance-based fee structure that would reward or share in any cost savings that were achieved by the Management Company.

Appendix J – Administration

Background:

Much has been written about how to cut operating costs through "waste elimination" and other techniques but not about how to apply disciplined cost reduction thinking to overhead functions, including finance, human resources, IT, legal, and administration. No company can sustain long-term results, without tackling these areas.

Administration costs are incurred to conduct the normal business activities of a condo or homeowner association and are not readily identified with a specific project or item. Most of these activities involve the storing, retrieving, integrating, and eventually disseminating of information to association members or the BoD. The two most significant cost opportunities arise whenever someone's time is involved or when there are paper transactions. Notices, requests, updates, communications, meeting agenda/minutes, inquiries, filings, documentation, and other forms of paperwork and document management all come at a cost. So do questions from members, follow-up responses, handling of suggestions/complaints, meetings/appointments, general questions (where to go or who to see), etc. It is in the best interest of the association to handle all of this expense in the most efficient and cost-effective manner possible, which is the reason why administration can be a fertile area of cost-reduction opportunity.

Most of the preferred solutions take advantage of the rapid advances in digital technology, computers, databases, digital documents, the Internet, and electronic communication. They also tend to operate on a "pull system" whereby users only "pull" the specific information that is being requested by them, rather than having someone else provide or "push" the information to them on a real time basis. Some examples of this include; information contained on an association website, newsletters, automate phone answering system, automatic check withdrawal, calendaring, automated reservations, etc. Technologies such as web meetings, teleconferencing, email/voice mail, cell phones/Blackberry/iPhone, Personal Digital Assistants (PDA), etc. can take advantage of handling business activities when people are at different locations and during different times.

Data and Pertinent Information:

- All of the typical association Secretary duties are areas of cost-savings opportunity including:
    - Safekeeping of the condo association non-financial clerical records and correspondence.
    - Prepares and sends out meeting notifications for Board and condo association meetings
    - Maintains minutes and required documentation on all meetings and distributes minutes, as required
    - Maintains all official records, including official correspondence, contracts, membership roster and contact information, certain historical documents, etc.
    - Receives, verifies, and maintains designation of co-owner's voting representative and proxies
    - Maintains a log of proposed resolutions, requested decisions, and decision outcomes
    - Establishes/maintains an emergency contact system for condo or homeowner association members
    - Maintains and communicates a Calendar of Key Events for Board and association members
- Most methods for addressing association document management involve the following.

Location	Where will documents be stored? Where will people need to go to access documents? Physical journeys to filing cabinets and file rooms are analogous to the onscreen navigation required to use a document management system.
Filing	How will documents be filed? What methods will be used to organize or index the documents to assist in later retrieval?
Retrieval	How will documents be found? Typically, retrieval encompasses both browsing through documents and searching for specific information.
Security	How will documents be kept secure? How will unauthorized personnel be prevented from reading, modifying or destroying documents?
Disaster Recovery	How can documents be recovered in case of destruction from fires, floods or natural disasters?
Retention period	How long should documents be kept, i.e. retained?
Archiving	How can documents be preserved for future readability?
Distribution	How can documents be available to the people that need them?
Workflow	If documents need to pass from one person to another, what are the rules for how their work should flow?
Creation	How are documents created? This question becomes important when multiple people need to collaborate, and the logistics of version control and authoring arise.
Authentication	Is there a way to vouch for the authenticity of a document?

- Many association governing documents were developed years ago without the benefit of technologies such as email, web pages, electronic meetings, etc. They should be revised, if needed, to take advantage of these improvements.

- More BoD's are relying heavily on the Web and electronic information to run their business. From a practical standpoint, volunteer BoD members may find it difficult to personally attend BoD meetings, due to other time commitments or geographical proximity. Electronic communication allows them to correspond via emails and through other

Web related tools, when they are available and without regard to where they are physically located. For a multitude reasons, it is strongly recommended that the Boards rely extensively upon electronic communications, the Web, and the associated tools to help them conduct their business and to supplement face-to-face meetings. You should thoroughly review your state laws and association governing documents to verify that you can use these technologies. Consider changing any association governing documents that prohibit you from doing so.

- In addition to a quicker response time, one of the main advantages of modern technology is that residents and unit owners are also often reachable 24/7. This is especially helpful in any kind of urgent situation for which the unit occupant is not home. Most association members owners have cell phones and can easily be reached at a moments notice. In addition to quicker response times in many cases, increased connectivity has also improved security and protection of the association facilities/assets. Security cameras can monitor who is entering and exiting the premises. Automated call systems can notify someone when there is a power outage, when a fire alarm goes off, when there is water intrusion, or if the inside room temperature is in danger of reaching a freeze level during the winter.

- Typically, a large expense for an association is collecting fees. Every month checks, money orders, or cash has to be received, processed, recorded, and deposited in a bank. If payments are not received, follow up letters or emails must be sent, often several times. All of this takes someone's time and effort which translates into cost.

- Consistent and effective communication in an association is extremely important to build consensus, distribute information, and to keep the rumor mill at bay. While printed newsletters have been the norm in the past, the web offers a wonderful alternative to publish newsletters on-line and eliminate printing, mailing, labeling, and postage costs. The same applies to distribution of meeting minutes and association.

- Instead of having to call someone to submit a maintenance request or architectural approval request, there are automated systems available where they can submit the request on a web site. Residents without computers can perform the same functions through an automated call center. A maintenance request or architectural approval request can go to the designated association manager, or in the case of a maintenance request, directly to the vendor under contract for repair services. If the repair is not the association's responsibility, the system will let the homeowner know. Association members can also electronically make arrangements to hook up sewer and water, arrange snow removal service and check their association account twenty-fours a day, seven days a week.

- A BoD or Management Company can get inundated with requests, inquiries, and complaints at all hours of the day/night from association members. Handling each of them requires their time, which is one of their most precious commodities and usually in short supply. This is an extremely inefficient way to handle the transfer of common information when it could be made available on an association website.

- Association websites can be developed and maintained at minimal cost to a condo or homeowner association. These websites can be invaluable in the dissemination of information to the members of the association and can contain financial information, on-line newsletters, rules and regulations, architectural guidelines, and governing documents as well as other information that the Board would like to pass on to the membership. All these items can be made available 24 hours a day, 7 days a week to owners, real estate agents, lenders, title companies, prospective buyers or anyone else that has a need to know. This saves the association time and money by eliminating the need to provide documents or answer calls. Instead, when information is requested, they are simply directed to the association website where they can copy or print out whatever they want, when they want it! Every question answered via the website is a question the BoD does not have to answer or pay their Management Company to answer.

- Condo or homeowner association websites have been met with mixed results. If you have a dull one that is not regularly refreshed with interesting information that people want to read about, it will probably not be well used. Some proven techniques include the following:

  – Show lots of pictures with "people" in them. Members love to read interesting things about their neighbors. Look for opportunities to highlight real people enjoying the facilities (special gatherings, normal day-to-day use, etc.). Whenever possible, post pictures of members performing volunteering efforts to point out contributions that are being made and to serve as an informal reward system for them. People pictures can be used to introduce a new asset, improvement, or feature. For example, rather than just showing a new pool filter that was purchased, you could show several members discussing the new pool filter that was just installed. Feature articles of members, their families, hobbies, special achievements, etc, can be a huge magnet to draw members to your website.

  – Another "draw" for members to come to the website is to publish area news that may be of interest to them. Scan daily local newspapers and Internet news for things like; impending legislation, changes in the property tax assessment, sightings of unique wildlife, special events, new bike riding trails, fall color tours in the area, increases in water/sewer/trash collection, etc. So, it makes it very convenient for them to simply go to the website to get the latest area news that impacts their association, rather than finding it out themselves.

– To make the best use of your website you must push information to your members and pull them to the site. This can easily be done by sending an email to members briefly telling them of important news or a developing situation that impacts them and then directing them to the website for a full explanation. This prompts them to visit the site and hopefully explore all other useful areas.

Recommendations/Alternatives to Be Considered:

• Store all the association's records in electronic form – Storage of the association's records can be both a space and money drain. It is not easy finding a place to securely store meeting minutes, bank records, and correspondence that goes back years and years. An easy solution is to store these documents in electronic form. Although original copies of some documents should be retained, all documents should be digitized for easy categorization and retrieval. Existing documents and are not in electronic form can be scanned. Make sure to keep multiple copies, in case of damage or destruction.

• Use e-mail for correspondence – One of the easiest steps you can take toward going paperless is to start using e-mail for most of your Association's communication. You can use e-mails for corresponding at the individual level or with group distribution lists. Depending on what your covenants/bylaws and state/local government rules state, you may also use e-mail to distribute the annual budget or notify owners of covenant violations and overdue assessments.

   – Individuals – Handling inquiries or responses, notifying owners of covenant violations, overdue fees, discussing opinions or requesting input from BoD members or association members, emergency individual notification, etc.

   – Group - Distributing a community newsletter or homeowner directory, communicating information on news and events taking place in the association, soliciting feedback on future BoD issues or decisions to be made, decisions that have been made by the BoD, emergency association notification, meeting notices and minutes, financial and legal information, useful information, etc.

- Maintain an association website – As almost all of an association's documents can be made accessible on-line, this is probably the biggest step you can take toward going paperless. An effective website can contain viewable and downloadable copies of all of the association's material records, such as its governing documents, meeting minutes, financial statements, permits, insurance policy, committee structure, business processes, and annual budget. It can also contain forms, such as architectural review requests, maintenance requests, community room reservations, which an owner can fill-out and submit to the BoD/Management Company electronically. A website may also contain copies of the association's newsletter, a homeowner directory, an event calendar, a community bulletin board. All of these features significantly reduce the need for paper, as well as increase an owner's ability to become involved in the community. An HOA Website is probably the best move your HOA can make to improve efficiency and reduce its administration costs. See *Appendix K* for a sample web site map for a small to medium size association.

  - To help ensure success of your website, you will not only need to "publicize" your website in nearly every conversation with owners, but to also constantly re-direct requests for information to the website. For example, when someone asks about: meeting minutes,
  governing documents, names of vendors, phone number of other owners, forms or templates, links to useful websites, etc., you're reply should be, "Oh yes, that information is on our website. It's on the xxxxx page or menu item".

- Consider on-line meetings for your BoD and/or annual meetings - Depending upon your geographical situation, governing documents, and state/local laws, you may be able to capitalize on the many electronic meeting choices that are available. In an on-line environment, people can interact with a group regardless of the participant's physical location; or one person can give a presentation or demonstration while the other participants become the audience. Attendance quorums can be easily achieved. In its simplest form, a telephone conference service (teleconferencing) can be used. For those members who are unable to be physically present, they log in via their own computer at the specified time and the meeting begins. The meeting is conducted as it normally would, except that you can not see the people in the room. Meeting information and documents are e-mailed prior to the meeting for reference purposes. More supplicated electronic meeting options include video-conferencing, real-time whiteboard or file transfers, on-line document collaboration, etc.
- Take advantage of automatic bill paying from both directions – Establish electronic capability to notify and collect association fees. Members who set up automatic bill paying seldom default. From the association standpoint, have vendors (utilities, lawn care, pool maintenance, etc.) automatically paid from the association account. It is in the best interest of the association to use these paperless-based bill paying alternatives.
- Handle maintenance & repair and architectural variance requests electronically – All requests should be in writing and then, depending upon the level of sophistication that is desired, use faxed copies, on-line submittal, e-mails, etc. to request and follow-up on items requiring action.
- Use on-line scheduling programs to reserve clubhouse/rooms, appointments, tennis courts dinner reservations, visitor parking passes, etc.

- Request Electronic Invoices from Vendors – You can request that your vendors bill you directly via e-mail. Many are now able and happy to do this, as it cuts down on their paper use as well. Electronic invoices can also be stored in a secure section of your association's website, making them available for inspection by the BoD.

- Utilize Internet Voting – Although the technology is still somewhat new, there are services available that allow your association to conduct its member voting on-line. If your governing documents allow this type of vote, all you need to do is supply the servicing company with ownership information, the ballot issue(s) to be decided, and the start and end dates of the vote. Owners are supplied with a secure log-in and can vote from the comfort of their home. The company will forward the results to the BoD when the vote is complete. No more need for costly mailings and mail-in ballots.

- Use automated phone answering to answer common questions (hours of operation, breaking news, meeting notices, etc) or to direct the call to the correct person (maintenance & repair, reservation, violation, etc.). The use of an off-site answering service can eliminate the need for an on-site person taking up facility space and overhead such as a desk, telephone equipment, and office supplies.

Appendix K – Sample Association Site Map

1) Home page
   a) Welcome statement
   b) Association news
   c) Area news
   d) Association history
   e) Association pictures/album
   f) Calendar of events
   g) Weather map
   h) Contact information
   i) Legal disclaimer
2) BoD Information & Decisions
   a) BoD description
   b) BoD mission & values
   c) Meeting minutes
   d) Notice of decisions
   e) President letters
   f) Annual meeting presentations
3) Committees & Processes
   a) Committee description, charter, and members
   b) Key business processes
   c) Maintenance & repair
      i) Introduction
      ii) Maintenance responsibility matrix
      iii) Work evaluation of vendors
   d) Architectural variance decisions
   e) Covenants, conditions, & restrictions (CCR) decisions
4) Financial & Legal
   a) Annual budget
   b) Annual budget performance
   c) Reserve study & strategy
   d) Reserve fund performance
   e) Association fee structure
   f) Association collection process
   g) Master deed & by-laws
   h) Disclosure statement
   i) Association legal settlements
   j) Master insurance policy
   k) Association tax returns
   l) Year end audits
   m) Permits
   n) Loan information
5) Contacts & Useful Information
   a) Emergency contact information
   b) Emergency response plan
   c) Association contractor contact numbers

d) Frequently Asked Questions (FAQ)
e) Buyer purchase guidelines
f) Association living experience and expectations
g) Competitive assessments of other area associations
h) Owner profile information
i) Association/homeowner information & tips
  i) Winterization
  ii) Area utility rates
  iii) Local property tax information
  iv) Original paint colors
  v) Etc.
j) Forms
  i) Request for BoD decision
  ii) Maintenance & repair
  iii) Architectural variance or approval
  iv) Proxy
  v) Club house reservation
  vi) Etc.
k) Recommended providers
l) Useful links
  i) Weather
  ii) Area events
  iii) State/township/city information
  iv) Chamber of commerce
  v) Local airports, marinas, etc.

Appendix L – Utilities

Background:

Utility costs vary substantially and can be a major cost to any condo or homeowner association. An association with few facilities may have minimal utility costs, while an apartment-style condominium may be responsible for all the electric, natural gas, water and sewer expenses in the complex and find utility costs a significant portion of its budget. Savings can often be realized by carefully analyzing utility usage and eliminating waste. To cut utility costs an association BoD should use some of the same energy saving practices home owners employ. This will most normally apply to the common elements of an association.

Data and Pertinent Information:

- Common element utilities for a condo or homeowner association could involve the following
    - Electricity
    - Natural gas
    - Water
    - Sewer service
    - Trash collection
- If the electricity service in a development is master-metered, the electric company bills the association for the total electricity consumed through the master meter. The hope is that residents will use these utilities prudently and conserve them by keeping the fixtures that dispense them in optimal working condition. Not so. Take water, for example: While association water bills continue to ratchet up, residents too often let dripping faucets and trickling toilets become background noise. The same principle applies to other association paid utilities. Lights are

often left on when no one's home. It is basic human nature: I'm not paying (directly) for it, so who cares? This lack of concern causes resources and dollars to literally go down the drain. Such systems may be eligible for bulk rate electricity depending upon the size of the community served and the amount of electricity consumed.

- The association might consider the feasibility of sub-metering to make each household responsible for its own electrical usage. Sub-metering (or individual metering) allocates electrical usage to those responsible and tends to promote energy conservation. Submetering is a cost-effective, efficient and highly effective way to promote electricity conservation and control costs. Submetering is also fair. Residents pay for the electricity they use. Conservers pay less while energy "hogs" pay more. Under a bulk metering system, the energy savers actually subsidize the cost of electricity for energy wasters and provide no incentive to reduce energy use. Research shows that when consumers pay for the electricity they use, the overall consumption of energy goes down. In fact, studies have shown that when submetering is installed in multi-unit complexes, electricity consumption is reduced by as much as 25 percent. That's good news for condominium BoD wanting to reduce overall costs. With submetering, the association is responsible for reading each unit's meter, preparing the bills, and collecting reimbursement monies due to the association.

- Individual metering refers to the installation of a meter in each unit by the electric company, making each household a residential customer. The electric company reads the meters, bills each household, handles service complaints, etc., and the association is billed as a separate customer only for the electricity used in the common areas and facilities. If the electric service in a residential association is master-metered and the association wants to convert to individual metering, the association is responsible for the costs incurred for rewiring or retrofitting and for the individual meters. Such conversion to individual metering in a master-metered building can be costly, and it is suggested that an association contact its electric utility for assistance when conducting a cost and feasibility analysis for individual metering.

- Remember also that if you're on a water meter and you are also on a municipal sewer system, your sewer bill is very likely calculated, according to water usage. So, the more water you use the high your sewer costs.

- The prime areas for saving money are in the parts of your association are common areas where energy is used 24 hours a day. Stairwell lighting, hallway lighting, and generator room lighting are just a few examples of where energy-efficient bulbs can be used to trim energy usage and save money. Illuminated exit signs are an important and legally required safety feature in your facility. In the case of an emergency such as a fire, their operation is critical in protecting the well being of your congregation's members. By design, exit signs operate 24 hours per day, and can consume large amounts of energy to operate. Many exit signs in today's buildings use older, incandescent and fluorescent/compact fluorescent lighting (CFL) technology. To make matters worse, many older exit signs require frequent maintenance due to the short life span of the lamps that light them. For example, many older exit signs consume over 350 kilowatt-hours (kWh) and cost $28 each annually to operate. The high-energy usage and maintenance of many exit signs is completely unnecessary due to advances in lighting technology. Solid-state light-emitting diodes (LED) are those small colored lights that have been used extensively in consumer electronics for decades. However recent advances in the technology have allowed exit sign manufacturers to develop signs that harness the advantages of this technology at competitive costs. LED exit signs use approximately 44 kWh of electricity annually to operate. Low energy use not only means less pollution but also lower electricity bills as a LED exit sign usually costs less than $4 annually to operate.

- ᵤwitching from traditional light bulbs (called incandescent) to Compact Fluorescent Light Bulbs (CFLs) is an effective, simple change that an association can make right now. CFLs use up to 75 percent less energy (electricity) than incandescent light bulbs, last up to 10 times longer, cost little up front, and provide a quick return on investment.

- An energy audit from a qualified professional usually consists of a thorough on-site survey of the premises when warranted, inspecting metering equipment and examining the specific usage of each service. Then, using an extensive tariff library and proprietary software that automatically flags billing errors and compares alternative rate structures, analysts work to obtain the maximum refunds and secure the lowest rates.

- The most expensive association amenities to offer on an ongoing basis are the wet amenities -- the pool, sauna, Jacuzzi or spa.

- Neglected landscaping and closed pools, tennis courts, golf courses and playgrounds erode already declining values and make it even harder to sell vacant units. Experts warn that a BoD's failure to properly maintain buildings and systems can send an association into a downward spiral.

Recommendations/Alternatives to Be Considered:

- **Perform an energy audit**. Associations with high utility costs should commission a utility audit to be conducted through their local utility company or third party contractor. It's important for an association to get a clear picture of their building's energy usage and learn what policies they might implement to help save them money. The most practical way to do this is by having an energy audit. Aside from identifying physical aspects of a building's energy profile, an energy audit also looks at the less tangible things. Every component of every utility bill should be carefully scrutinized for accuracy in order to uncover and eliminate hidden overcharges. Furthermore, a thorough comparison of current costs against alternative rate structures based on the association building's equipment and load profile should be made in order to take advantage of every available billing reduction opportunity. To simply assume that utility bills are accurate and that the utility companies are charging the lowest rates available can be a costly mistake.

- **Reduce inside water consumption** – Inside water retrofit strategies that involve relatively modest investments and quick paybacks from savings on water and sewer bills include:
  - **Low-flow faucet aerators.** Screw-on aerators for bathroom and kitchen faucets are generally available in hardware stores for under $2. Property managers or residents can install the aerators with minimum effort. Aerators may save from half a gallon to over 4.5 gallons per faucet per day.
  - **Low-flow showerheads.** Low-flow showerheads (flow rate of 2.5 gallons per minute or lower) are available for as little as $2, although some of the fancier models can cost upward of $20. Their installation involves unscrewing the old showerhead and replacing it with the low-flow model. The replacement of non-conserving showerheads with low-flow fixtures may save between 3 and 6 gallons per showerhead per day.
  - **Toilet inserts.** Three types of toilet inserts can be implemented at relatively low cost.
    - **Displacement devices** (blocks or bottles placed inside the toilet tank to take up space formerly occupied by water) can be purchased for under one dollar; installation requires only the lifting of the toilet tank lid and the placement of the device inside the tank. Displacement devices may save from 1 to 3 gallons per toilet per day; they should only be used in toilets with large tanks (5 gallons or more).

- **Quick-closing flapper.** The flapper valve inside the toilet tank (the device that lifts up to allow water from the tank into the bowl) can be replaced with a quick-closing flapper designed to clamp down before the tank is emptied. Flapper valves cost between $2 and $10 and take a plumber or handyman under 20 minutes to install. They may save between 2 to 4 gallons per day per retrofitted toilet.

- **Water level adjustments.** The water level in the toilet tank can be adjusted to use less water per flush. Water level adjustments can best be accomplished using a dual-flush adapter, a device that provides for short or long flushes. Adapters may cost between $8 and $20 and take about 20 minutes to install. Water level adjustments may save from 1 to 3 gallons per toilet per day.

– **Leak detection and repair.** Toilet, faucet, and showerhead leaks are easy to detect and repair. The repair of faucets and showerheads generally involves a gasket replacement (costs under one dollar), which a handyman can perform in under 15 minutes. Toilets usually leak because of defective flapper valves; flapper valves can be installed for $10 or less in under 20 minutes (the appropriate flapper for the toilet model should be used or leaking may continue). The water savings from leak repairs can be significant. Severe leaks, more common in toilets than in other fixtures, can drain over 100 gallons per day. Even modest leaks can lose 3 to 7 gallons per day per toilet and about a gallon per day per faucet or showerhead.

– **Utility-financed strategies**

- Toilets through direct-install programs. Many water utilities across the country have recognized the water savings potential of ultra-low flush toilets (ULFT) and offer incentives to replace old toilets with water conserving fixtures. ULFTs are toilets designed to use 1.6 gallons per flush or less, compared to the 3.5 gallons per flush or higher in toilets manufactured before 1992. ULFTs can save between 10 to 20 gallons per toilet per day.

- Devices through water conservation kits. Many water utilities in the United States offer water conservation kits to customers in their service areas. The kits generally include two or three faucet aerators, a low-flow showerhead, toilet displacement devices, leak detection tablets for toilets, and informational materials. Property owners should undertake installation of the water conserving devices with their own personnel, rather than leave it up to the residents to obtain the full water savings from the free devices.
- Rebates. A number of utilities promote the use of ultra low flush toilets and high efficiency clothes washers through rebate programs. The details of each program vary from one location to the next.

– **Submetering.** Submetering refers to the installation of water meters on the water supply lines to each apartment. The meters track the water consumption of each unit, and the residents are responsible for their own water bills. Water is thus billed according to the amount consumed — the same fashion that electricity and gas have been billed for years. There may be regulations on local or state water codes that prohibit sub-metering. Property owners have several options when considering a submetering system:

- Hire a large company with offices nationwide
- Hire a local contractor specialized in submetering services
- Implement the systems on their own, as some of the larger property owners have done
- Request direct utility metering at apartment or condo units
- Use a combination of the above.

- The cost of implementing a submetering system may vary among regions of the country and even from one property to the next. The way water piping is laid out in a building can impact costs. The total cost must also include the billing and collection processes, handling of customer complaints, increased maintenance requirements, and interaction with the local water utility. Based on limited data, implementation costs may range between $225 and $500 per unit. Operation and maintenance costs may fall between $2 and $3 per month per unit. The volume of water saved by the implementation of a submetering system will depend on the cost of water, location, income level, age of residents, etc. It is not uncommon to achieve water savings between 20 and 30 percent of total use with submetering systems.

  – **Pressure reduction.** Because flow rate is related to pressure, the maximum water flow from a fixture operating on a fixed setting can be reduced if the water pressure is reduced. For example, a reduction in pressure from 100 pounds per square inch to 50 psi at an outlet can result in a water flow reduction of about one-third. Condos and homeowner can reduce the water pressure in common element facilities by installing pressure-reducing valves. The use of such valves might be one way to decrease water consumption in homes that are served by municipal water systems. For associations served by wells, reducing the system pressure can save both water and energy.

- **Reduce outside water consumption.** Outdoor retrofit strategies involve improving irrigation efficiency and limiting outside water uses. Several effective means of reducing water consumption are described below.

  – **Eliminate narrow turf strips.** The volume of water saved by eliminating narrow strips of turf will depend on the size of the area in question and the material that replaces the lawn: paving/gravel (no water use), or plants/shrubs (some water use). Water savings and costs must be estimated on a case-by-case basis. One study conducted in Novato, California, showed narrow strips of turf required about four times the amount of water per square foot applied on larger turf areas. Actual water savings will vary in different parts of the country.

— **Reduce lawn areas.** Smaller lawns save water and may reduce maintenance costs. This is particularly true in arid and semi-arid areas where the volume of water used in irrigation can represent a significant proportion of the total water consumption. The water savings and costs associated with reducing lawn areas depend on the size of the area in question and the material that replaces the lawn: paving/gravel, attractive boulders, or plants/ shrubs. Water savings from a reduction in turf areas would only accrue during the period the lawn is irrigated.

— **Use separate water meters.** While the meters themselves do not save water, property owner/manager appreciation of the amounts of water used for common areas may prompt them to implement one or more measures to improve outdoor water use efficiency. Reductions in water use of 5 to 10 percent from the use of separate meters are feasible, although actual savings need to be evaluated on a case-by-case basis.

— **Install soil moisture or rain sensors.** Soil moisture sensors/probes or rain sensors can save 5 to 10 percent of water used outdoors, provided the moisture/rainfall data are used to adjust irrigation schedules. The cost of implementing moisture or rain sensors will vary depending on the type and quality of devices used. Rain sensors typically cost around $25; installation may take an hour of plumber time and maintenance costs are minimal. Moisture sensors can range from $10 for a simple resistance probe to $75 or more for a tensiometer, a device that measures soil moisture tension by quantifying the amount of water a plant can draw from the soil.

— **Install special hose bibs.** Hose bibs or outdoor faucets may be retrofitted with attachments that require a special key to use the outlet. The retrofit costs under $10 and may be installed in a few minutes by a plumber or handyman. The volume of water saved by restricting use of outdoor faucets/hose bibs will be site specific. Properties where owners frequently wash cars on the premises would benefit most from implementation of this strategy. Water use can be reduced by 50 percent or more at each retrofitted hose bib.

— **Replace sprinklers with drip irrigation.** Drip irrigation systems can save 25 to 75 percent of the water that a sprinkler system would use. Actual savings must be determined on a case-by-case basis, and depend on the type of sprinklers replaced and the characteristics of the irrigated area. The cost of replacing sprinklers with a drip system depends on the size of the area to be irrigated and the type of system installed. The cost of installing a drip system is estimated at $1 to $1.50 per square foot. Drip systems do require periodic maintenance for efficient operation.

— **Landscape with native plants.** The volume of water saved by using low-water use and native plants in place of conventional landscaping needs to be evaluated on a case-by-case basis. Replacing conventional landscapes with low water use and native plants can reduce outdoor water up to 40%, depending on the location, type of plants replaced, and irrigation system efficiency. Estimated installation costs are $1 to $4 per square foot and the cost of the native plants can vary from $2 to nearly $100 per plant. An approximate cost of $2 per square foot of area to be planted may be used as a rough "rule of thumb" estimate. Operation and maintenance costs should actually decrease with the native plants, as they are better adapted to local conditions than less water efficient plants.

- **Increase gray water conservation.** The least traditional retrofit strategy for water conservation in a condo or homeowner association setting is the installation of gray water systems. Gray water systems may consist of:

  - Rainwater collection
  - Gray water recycling
  - Hybrid rainwater collection and recycling systems

- In terms of cost effectiveness, hybrid systems rank higher than the other two alternatives. Gray water recycling tends to be more cost effective than rainwater collection.

- **Reduce electricity consumption.** It's hard to imagine life without electricity. In our homes, we rely on it to power our lights, appliances, and electronics. When trying to reduce electrical consumption, attack the biggest energy-users first. You'll save more electricity by dealing with the biggest electricity-guzzlers rather than worrying about items that don't use much electricity.

  - **Air conditioner.** In the typical home, air conditioning uses more electricity than anything else -- 16% of total electricity used. In warmer regions AC can be 60-70% of your summer electric bill. If you're serious about saving energy, address your cooling costs first, since that's what uses the most electricity. Of course, you'll save the most money if you can learn to do without your AC at all.

    - Raise the temperature. Each degree below 78 will increase your energy use by 3-4%.
    - Install ceiling fans if you don't have them. Fans can make the temperature seem 10 degrees cooler, drastically reducing your need for AC. Don't underestimate the importance of ceiling fans. Make sure your fan is blowing DOWN, to send air past your body, removing the hot air that

surrounds your body. If your fan is blowing up, it won't do any good. In fact, it will make you warmer by bouncing the warm air that collects at the ceiling back down towards the living area.

- Use a timer or thermostat to turn off about the time you leave for the day, and to turn back on a half hour before you get home. Contrary to popular belief, this does NOT use more electricity than having the AC constantly maintain a cool temperature; it uses less.

- Close the registers in unused rooms. If you have central AC you can close registers in rooms you're not using so you're not paying to cool them.

- **Heat pump.** Heat Pumps require annual checkups to maintain peak efficiency. Research shows that if your refrigerant level is just 10% less than what it should be, your system's efficiency can be decreased up to 50%. Consider obtaining a service agreement with a licensed air conditioning contractor or dealer to assure peak efficiency of your heat pump.

- **Heating (if you have electric heat).** There are four main strategies to save money on heat

  - Heat only the parts of your home that you're using. Heating your whole house is more expensive than heating just part of it.

  - Adjust your living environment so that you're comfortable at lower temperatures. This includes using ceiling fans.

  - Use cheap or efficient heating systems. Choose between heat pumps vs. oil/gas, and radiant vs. forced-air.

  - Insulate your home well to keep heat from escaping out of the house. You want to pay only to heat your home, not the outside. This includes things like weather stripping doors and windows.

- **Hot water heater.** Old-style tank water heaters are wasteful because they have to keep the water hot 24/7 whether you're using any water or not.

  - Go tankless. The modern replacement is a tankless unit, which heats the water instantly when you turn on the faucet. You can choose either gas or electric, just like with an old tank heater, and either way you'll save money over a tank heater.

  - Turn down the thermostat. When it's set on scalding hot you have to mix in cold water in your shower to lower the temperature, and why make your heater boil the water if you don't need it that hot? For each 10°F reduction in water temperature, you can save between 3%–5% in energy costs.

  - Wrap your heater in a special tank blanket. Home improvement stores sell a special water heater blanket that you can put around your heater to help insulate it. This reduces energy use by 10-15%

- **Lighting.**

  - Replace your incandescent bulbs with Compact fluorescent lamps (CFL) which last six to 10 times longer and are much more efficient. A CFL uses 75% less electricity than an incandescent bulb to produce the same amount of light—so a 15-watt CFL is just as bright as a 60-watt incandescent. (CFLs) are more expensive but pay for themselves with energy savings. You can also save energy by installing photocells on outdoor lights. Exterior lighting is one of the best places to use CFLs because of their long life. In addition to the energy savings, you don't have to pay to have bulbs replaced as frequently.

- Replace all exit signs with LED exit signs that use approximately 44 kWh of electricity annually to operate. Low energy use not only means less pollution but also lower electricity bills as a LED exit sign usually costs less than $4 annually to operate.
- Replace all outside lights with energy efficient bulbs (CFL or sodium vapor)

- **Heating Gas – Forced Air.** Furnace Filters should be checked every two weeks during cooling seasons and every month during heating season. Dirty filters should be cleaned or replaced.

- **Insulation and weatherization.**
  - An association can reduce their heating and cooling needs by up to 30 percent by investing a few hundred dollars in proper insulation and weatherization. This is one of the easiest and most cost-efficient ways to reduce energy waste and maximize energy dollars. Insulation is measured in R-values. The higher the R- value, the better the walls and roof will resist the transfer of heat and cold. There should be a minimum of R-22 (seven inches of fiber glass or rock wool or six inches of cellulose). Most homes have between R-22 and R-49 insulation in the attic.
  - Caulk, seal and weather-strip all seams, cracks and openings to the outside. Reducing air leaks can save up to ten percent of the electricity bill.

- **Swimming pool/spa**
  - **Heating.** Heating a swimming pool/spa can consume a lot of energy and add up to high heating bills. You can improve your swimming pool's heating and energy efficiency by doing the following:
    - Installing a high efficiency or solar pool heater. You have a lot to consider when selecting a new water heater. You should choose a water heating system that will not only provide enough hot water but also that will do so energy

efficiently, saving you money. This includes considering the different types of water heaters available and determining the right size and fuel source for your pool/spa.

- Using a pool cover. Swimming pools lose energy in a variety of ways, but evaporation is by far the largest source of energy loss. Pool covers minimize evaporation from both outdoor and indoor pools. Covering a pool when it is not in use is the single most effective means of reducing pool heating costs. Savings of 50%–70% are possible. Besides offering energy savings, pool covers also do the following:
    - Conserve water by reducing the amount of make-up water needed by 30%–50%
    - Reduce the pool's chemical consumption by 35%–60%
    - Reduce cleaning time by keeping dirt and other debris out of the pool.

- Managing the water temperature. The energy consumption for each degree rise in temperature will cost 10%–30% more in energy costs, depending on your location. Also, turn the temperature down or turn off the heater whenever the pool won't be used for several days. This will save energy and money. It's a myth that it takes more energy to heat a pool back up to a desired temperature than you save by lowering the temperature or turning off the heater.

- Installing a smaller, energy-efficient pump and/or operating it less. The larger the pump, the greater your pumping and maintenance costs. Therefore, you want to use the smallest size pump possible for your swimming pool. Pool pumps often run much longer than necessary. Circulating your pool's water keeps the chemicals mixed and removes debris. However, as long the water circulates while chemicals are added, they should remain mixed. Reduce your filtration time to 6 hours per day. If the water doesn't appear clean, increase the time in half-hour increments until it does. In the Florida study, most people who reduced pumping to less than 3 hours per day were still happy with the water's quality. On average, this saved them 60% of their electricity bill for pumping.

- You can install a timer to control the pump's cycling. If debris is a problem, use a timer that can activate the pump for many short periods each day. Running the pump continuously for, say, 3 hours leaves the other 21 hours a day for the pool to collect debris. Several short cycles keep the pool cleaner all day.

- Closure. That pool or spa may be used by only a hand full of residents and cost up to 20% of the annual budget. If an appropriate majority can legally approve shutting it down, major money could be saved.

Appendix M – Insurance

Background:

All condo and homeowner associations are vulnerable to the loss of property and finances, thus the need for insurance. Simply put, insurance equals protection. Insurance will help protect your investment if your building is damaged or destroyed by fire or other causes. Public liability coverage will protect you if someone is hurt in the building and sues you. Insurance is vital to the financial stability of an association because without it, one big loss can place an association in financial turmoil.

Since BoD members have a fiduciary duty to protect association assets, its insurance program is the keystone to asset protection. As a rule, all associations should have Fire & Hazard, Directors & Officers Liability, Fidelity and General Liability coverages. Some other desirable coverages include Earthquake (mandatory in some regions) and Building Ordinance or Law. The latter covers increased reconstruction costs due to building code or zoning restrictions. Earthquake insurance typically has a sizeable deduction, like 10% of the coverage amount. Owners must carry insurance at their own expense to insure their separate interests.

Association insurance is a major expense item. Decisions to reduce an association's insurance cost and buying the correct insurance policy is not a one-step process, but is the end product of a series of investigations the BoD has to make about how to protect association assets. Those steps include identifying the risks and then eliminating, transferring, or assuming those risks. One underlying principle to keep in mind is that insurance in any form presents some form of risk for the insured. The gamble is that bad things won't happen but insurance companies know that somewhere, sometime, they will. When insurance pays off, the costs impact the premium rate structure for an association. So, during tight insurance markets, the BoD will need to consider increasing the association's risk to reduce premium cost.

Data and Pertinent Information:

- The insurance industry periodically goes through what is known as a "hard market" meaning that insurance premiums are on the rise, coverage is harder to obtain, and policies include more limitations and exclusions. The realities of a hard market have a significant impact on condo and homeowners associations that could result in the following:
  - Increased insurance premiums. It is not uncommon for annual increases of 20% to 25% and some have experienced increases of 100%. The rise in premiums may be less extreme in smaller communities.
  - Associations are more likely to be non-renewed if they have bad loss ratios and/or multiple claims. Also, older buildings which lack adequate fire life safety protection may not be renewed.
  - Insurance policies come with more and more exclusions. Associations with a history of a particular kind of loss, such as annual flooding, may find themselves with exclusions in their coverage and/or particularly high premiums. Virtually all associations have found that their insurance policies do not cover damages for mold, terrorism or lead.
  - Many insurance companies are denying coverage if they are not notified of a possible claim in a timely manner. It has become very important for associations to report even the threat of a lawsuit as early as possible.
- Based upon the insurance company's inspections, they typically provide recommendations that range from "Critical," in which certain things must be done to the property in a particular timeframe; to "Important," in which things must be acted upon over the next year—to "We'd like you

to think about. Pay close attention to insurance company loss control recommendations on life safety and security issues. Things such as emergency lighting, hardwired or battery-operated smoke detectors in common areas, locked entrances and exits, and keeping sidewalks and walkways in excellent condition make a big difference. Ensuring that there is a panic bar on the door allowing access to the roof, and following regulations for elevators, gyms and laundry rooms also are important.

- New underwriting guidelines adopted recently by Fannie Mae and Freddie Mac (the entities that buy most home mortgage loans) require lenders to assess the financial strength of condo and homeowner associations as well as the credit of the borrowers purchasing units in them. Under the full project review now required for most condominium loans, lenders must verify and warrant to Fannie Mae that:
  - The homeowner association has an "adequate" budget.
  - The budget allocates at least 10% of annual revenues to reserves.
  - The condo or homeowner association holds funds equaling the deductible under the master insurance policy.
  - No more than 15% of the common area fees are delinquent by more than one month

- It is a well-known fact that associations with poor histories from numerous claims pay more in premiums than those with spotless pasts. Prior losses, liability lawsuits, windstorm damage, building vacancies and workmen's compensation payments are only some of the factors that can affect insurance premiums. A BoD can take pro-active measures to keep insurance bills as low as possible, while also assuring that the carrier will continue to insure the building after the current policy has expired.

- For years, certain aspects of insurance coverage have been view as sacred -- and therefore rarely tinkered with during any insurance review. They may not be so sacred after all. For example, service-insurance

contract on boiler machinery and other mechanical equipment.
Routinely renewed year after year, the money might better be spent
adding to reserves. Figured over the life of any item, premiums often
exceed the cost of replacing components or even the item itself.
Another area to look at is annual inflation adjustments. Although
inflation has been minimal in the construction trades, many insurance
companies still routinely add 10 percent a year as an inflation guard for
structural coverage. What you did 10 years ago may not be needed
anymore. To avoid overpayment, an accurate reassessment should
instead be made of current replacement costs.

Recommendations/Alternatives to Be Considered:

- **Closely examine your insurance policies.** Make sure you are
  adequately insured and/or have coverage in your policy which you may
  not need. Work with an insurance agent who has experience working
  with the specific needs of condo or homeowner's associations.
- **Raise the deductibles that will in turn reduce the annual premium.** The
  deductible you choose is also called the level of "self insurance." With
  any claim filed, the condo or homeowner will pay the deductible portion
  before the remaining balance is covered by the insurance. Because of
  the new Fannie Mae/Freddie Mac lending guidelines, the BoD may want
  set up a fund for insurance deductibles. The best way to handle the
  issue is to create a separate fund, but keep the monies in the same
  account as the reserves. Associations can have a line item in their
  budgets for "Insurance Deductible Fund" and contribute to the fund over
  several years until the deductible is fully funded. At that point, the
  contribution could be discontinued until an insurance claim is made, at
  which point the deductible would be replenished with new contributions.

As an alternative to increased premiums, some associations have opted to increase their deductible. While the typical deductible remains $1,000.00, many associations have raised their deductibles to $5,000.00 and $10,000.

- **Control your claims.** Be proactive about risk management. The best way to reduce premium costs is to limit the kind and frequency of insurance claims that you file. Do not put in every insurance claim, particularly if it is a small claim. Every claim goes on your loss run and that affects your premium. Insurance companies use past loss history (loss reports) for the past three to five years as an indication in a rating matrix. Many professionals believe that a condo or homeowner's insurance is something you don't want to use - it is there for catastrophic events. Use the association's reserve study to identify risks and quantify exposures. An older roof is more likely to be damaged in a severe storm and so represents a greater risk than a newer one.

- **At least every two years, competitively quote your insurance policy with a minimum of three providers.** Not all insurance carriers have experienced the same loss history and have lower premiums. Check with national companies that have a special line of condo or homeowner coverages like State Farm, Farmers and Community Association Underwriters for options. Ask for the agent that writes the greatest amount of association insurance. It's very important to only deal with an agent that is knowledgeable about how associations work. There are also a variety of independent insurance agents who can shop a wide market of companies to build a policy for you as well. If you are changing carriers and/or agents, ask the agent to certify in writing what the new policy covers. You want this statement to include an apples-to-apples comparison listing the coverage you had in the old policy, the coverage you are getting in the new policy that you did not have before, and the coverage you had previously that the new policy will not provide.

- **Directing claims to members' insurance will reduce claims on the association's insurance.** The association's insurance should typically be used for larger claims like wind, rain and fire damage that impact many units or other common area structures. Assuming the CC&Rs are silent on the issue, BoD's may adopt a policy that any loss attributable to an owner that results in a claim against the association's insurance, the owner shall pay the deductible. This is easy for owners to do if they have the deductible coverage that is an inexpensive addition to an owner's policy. Any such amendment should make it clear that owners pay the deductible when they are responsible for the loss, either because of their own negligence or because something under their control failed (such as a dishwasher, toilet valve, etc.) Tapping the owner's policy first is less costly for the association and makes the master policy do what it is supposed to do - insure the community against catastrophic losses.

- **Minimize the number of items which qualify for an association insurance claim.** A condo or homeowner association governing documents will spell out the insurance responsibilities for an association. However, there are likely many areas that are not addressed directly. The BoD should develop a Maintenance & Insurance Responsibility Matrix (*See Appendix N*) that spells out exactly who is responsible for what when it comes to maintenance responsibility and insurance coverage. Once completed, this responsibility matrix can be provided to the association and homeowner insurance carriers for them to identify any gaps that are not covered in their respective policies. If there are gaps, this is the time to close them. Also by doing this, Insurance agents are effectively put on notice.

- **Reduce insurance liabilities in your buildings.** Without hiring anyone from an outside source, any condo or homeowner's association can request a questionnaire from their insurance company that goes over common risks and exposures at the property. By filling out the questionnaire, a community association can quickly get a rough sketch of problem areas. Even better, most insurance companies will arrange a site visit by a risk assessment officer to the property. Many steps can be taken to lower a building's liability with minimal cost including:

- A poorly maintained parking lot is a common problem, particularly for older associations that still have the original pavement down. Typical problems found include potholes and a variety of cracks. All of these conditions can let water collect and lead to freeze-thaw cycles, which speed up wear and tear and create slip-and-fall hazards

- Another big slip-and-fall hazard results from downspouts which pour rainwater directly onto pavements. You should reroute downspouts or extend them so they empty their rainwater at least three to four feet away from the pedestrian walkways.

- Ensuring that all doors are locked at all times, particularly out of the way basement doors and rear entries, lowers liability and increases the safety of the residents. Each building also should practice good maintenance—no wet floors or trip/fall hazards

- On the water damage front, most exposure results from water heaters and washing machines. Water heaters more than five years old are at great risk of failing and causing a flood. The best route is to carefully note the date that the water heater was installed, then "watch it like a hawk" after the half-decade mark. The unit should then be replaced at the first sign of leakage.

- If possible, you should update your building's electric, plumbing and central air conditioning. Update junction boxes from fuses to circuit breakers. Plumbing updates will reduce risks in some older buildings by lowering the probability of pipes bursting and causing

expensive property damage. Make sure that your building's air
conditioning drain lines and pans also are kept clean.

— Be sure that any contractor that is doing work on the property is
properly insured. The contractor should have liability, worker's
compensation, umbrella insurance and auto insurance. You also
want an indemnification agreement.

— Installing sprinkler systems, burglar alarms and security cameras
can positively affect a building's insurance rating

— Taking life safety measures for a building is always helpful in
reducing insurance costs. One measure is to institute a fire safety
program, in which the building's occupants are taught how to exit
the building in the event of a fire.

— Insurance companies do an annual inspection of the property --
that's free advice. Those recommendations (of the insurance
company) should be taken seriously

Appendix N – Sample Maintenance Responsibility Matrix

Description	Assoc. Resp.	Owner's Resp.	Comments
• Air Conditioners:		X	Reference NOA00007
– Compressor		X	
– Duct Work		X	
– Fan		X	
• Animal/Birds (Stray)			
– In Unit		X	
– Inside Attic/Roof/Walls *(General insurance exclusion and limited coverage)*	X		
• Appliances:			Reference NOA00007
– Dishwasher		X	
– Microwave		X	
– Range Hood		X	
– Refrigerator		X	
– Stove		X	
– Water Heater		X	
– Washer and Dryer		X	
– Garbage Disposal		X	
– Gas Fireplace		X	
– Garage Door Opener		X	
– Furnace		X	
▪ Filter replacement		X	
▪ Condensate pump		X	
▪ Thermostat		X	
– Smoke Detector		X	
• Deck:			2007 Reserve Plan
– Decking material & structure (defects due to natural occurrences)	X		
– Power washing & mold control		X	
• Enclosed Porch:			

Item	Col 1	Col 2	Col 3
– Carpet/Tile/other surface treatments		X	
– Fixtures, Lights & Switches		X	
– Screens (defects due to natural occurrences)	X		
– Floor Structure (not surface treatment)	X		
– Frame, Exterior Trim & Sills	X		
• Chimney:			
– Birds		X	
– Cap Cracks	X		
– Cleaning		X	
– Flue		X	
– Leaks - Water	X		
• Driveways			2007 Reserve Plan
– Snow Removal	X		
– Repair and sealing	X		
• Sidewalk			
– Repair & Sealing		X	
– Snow Removal		X	
• Electrical:			
– Circuit Breakers		X	
– Circuits (wiring in walls)	X		
– Doorbells		X	
– Outside Deck			
▪ Fixture & Wiring	X		
▪ Bulb Replacement		X	
▪ Switches		X	
– Interior Outlets, Switches		X	
• Fences & Gates	X		
• Mail Boxes and Entrance Sign	X		
• Sewer Grinder Station	X		
• Landscaping			
– Common areas; lawn, retaining walls, landscaping stones, trees, shrubs, plants,	X		

	etc. maintenance & repair			
–	Common/Limited Common Area Fertilization, Weed Control	X		
–	Courtyard area grass, trees, shrubs, plants, sea grass, etc. maintenance & repair		X	
–	Common Areas Irrigation	X		
–	Courtyard Irrigation		X	
•	Entry Doors:			
–	Door Knob & Locksets		X	
–	Frame, Exterior Trim & Sills	X		
–	Interior & Exterior Surfaces		X	
–	Threshold	X		
–	Warping	X		
–	Weather Stripping		X	
•	Exterior			
–	General Maintenance	X		Any not specified elsewhere
–	Trim & Siding	X		
–	Gutters	X		2007 Reserve Plan
–	Foundation brick	X		
–	Water Damage	X		
–	Roof	X		
–	Chimneys & Vents	X		
–	Foundations	X		
–	Spider Control		X	
•	Garages:			2007 Reserve Plan
–	Inside Lights		X	
–	Outside Light Fixture & Wiring	X		
–	All Switches		X	
–	Walls (exterior)	X		
–	Doors Weather Stripping,		X	
–	Garage Doors (incl.		X	

	springs, tracks, hardware other than opener)			
–	Door Opener		X	
•	Windows/Glass Doors:			
–	Long-Term Replacement	X		2007 Reserve Plan
–	Broken Pane (defects due to natural occurrences)	X		
–	Broken Seal	X		
–	Caulking (exterior)	X		
–	Exterior Frame, Trim, & Sills	X		
–	Lock		X	
–	Screen		X	
–	Interior Sills		X	
–	Stuck		X	
–	Washing		X	
•	Interior:			
–	Cabinets, Shelves		X	
–	Carpet		X	
–	Ceiling		X	
–	Doors		X	
–	Drywall		X	
–	Floors		X	
–	Sub-floor		X	
–	Tile		X	
–	Trim		X	
–	Walls		X	
•	Plumbing:			
–	Drain Clogging		X	
–	Faucet - Exterior	X		
–	Faucet/Fixture - Interior		X	
–	Sewer Backup, Main Line	X		
–	Toilet		X	
–	Storm Sewers	X		
•	Utility Lines			
–	Electrical in Walls & Meter	X		
–	Water Lines in Walls & Meter	X		
–	Telephone Jack		X	
–	Telephone wiring in	X		

walls			
— TV Cable Jack		X	
— TV Cable in walls	X		

Appendix O – Purchased Services

Background:

Every year, condo and homeowner associations spend significant amounts of money on purchased goods and services unnecessarily. Suppliers price their offerings according to what the market will bear, and unless you let them know you won't bear it anymore, you will pay more than you have to. Rarely will a supplier volunteer a price reduction (even to its most valued customer) without some pressure from the customer or their competition. Let suppliers know you are reviewing your costs, which have to be reduced. Refuse to accept price increases and you will be surprised at the number of suppliers who back down. Noise without knowledge will get you only so far. Do your research before you approach suppliers so you can negotiate from a position of strength. During negotiations, present the value of your business to the supplier in the most favorable light possible. Finally, don't accept the supplier's statement, "Our prices are higher because we provide superior quality and service", without doing some comparison shopping.

Large service contracts like landscaping, property management, pool maintenance and janitorial services should be competitively bid a minimum of every two years. Even if you are totally satisfied with the service received and have no intention of changing provider, it will demonstrate to the membership that the BoD is practicing due diligence and good stewardship. Also, if a particular service provider is maneuvering for a contract increase, a competitive proposal will work to the association's advantage in negotiating or verifying that your current provider is entirely justified in the increase.

Data and Pertinent Information:

- Management of a community association's resources frequently involves the use of contracts to obtain the products and services required. Given such, one component of the BoD's fiduciary responsibility is to make sure that the association is not paying too much for the products and services it receives. The most effective way to ensure competitive prices is through bid requests to potential contractors. A bid request or request for proposal (RFP) is an announcement that an organization is interested in receiving proposals for a particular product or service. The bid request form includes: bid specifications (detailed instructions about the products or services requested); information about the association that the contractor will need in order to prepare a bid; and, a request for information about the contractor that will help the association evaluate the contractor's ability to perform the work and meet the specifications. This process should not only be used for common items such as maintenance & repair, construction, etc. but also for services such as Management Company, accounting, legal, pest control, locksmith and pond maintenance etc.

- It is suggested that you go into any supplier bidding process with a healthy dose of skepticism. Don't be negative and don't discount everything the supplier says, but certainly don't take everything that is said as gospel truth. Remember, the supplier representatives that show up at the bid meetings are usually marketing (sales) representatives. They will often over promise and have been taught to develop a relationship with the client, because it's easier to convince a "friend" to buy a product or service. There are three keys to a successful supplier relationship.

  – Write good specifications. Specifications are key to a successful contract and they must be included in the bid documentations.

  – Invite only prequalified suppliers to bid. Before you even invite a supplier to bid you must have prequalified them. You must confident that whoever wins the bid, will be a good choice. You should never be afraid of a certain supplier winning the bid.

- Make an educated decision on which supplier to select. Too many times a supplier decision based on just a couple of factors and often price at the top of that list. This can result in a low price but inferior service. This inferior service affects both the association and its members.

• One important cost factor is negotiating a fixed-price contract. With snow removal, for example, set a price for the season, not by the snowfall or how many inches are removed. Association properties are on pretty much a fixed budget and there's no sense going back to the owners and saying we need an assessment to pay for this season's storms that weren't put into the budget

• If you use a Management Company, an area that deserves close scrutiny for cost reduction is any routine services that may be provided. This includes such things as routine maintenance, security guards, office help, etc. What is the hourly charge for the services being provided? How does this compare for the local going rate for private contractors or apartment buildings? Do not let your Management Company bully you on this one by saying that it is not possible to directly hire someone to provide these services. It is possible and often advisable. This can be an area for a Management Company to get "healthy" at your expense, by charging you a high prevailing rate and paying the person at a much lower rate (i.e. – profit for them). If you use this strategy, there are a couple of considerations that you should be made aware of:

- If you hire a person as an employee to perform this function, under the law, you are required to pay payroll taxes, benefits, and workers compensation insurance. You also have the added administrative responsibility of keeping payroll records, generating payment checks, and filing income tax statements. A way to avoid this unpleasant administrative task is to have the payroll administered thru a payroll company (like ADP or Paychex). They will deal with the taxes, benefits, and insurance. All you will have to do is fax in 'timesheets' to the company and they prepare the payroll. You will get detailed information on your costs and thru electronic funds transfer, you can pay the company.

– Some associations only use independent contractors as a way to avoid payroll taxes, health benefits, and workers compensation insurance. To avoid misclassification of employees in the eyes of the government, associations should limit the use of "full-time" independent contractors, and instead hire workers on a specific project basis. Additionally, associations should treat workers similarly in similar situations. In other words, if the job duties of two employees are the same or similar, do not hire one as an independent contractor and the other as an employee.

Recommendations/Alternatives to Be Considered:

• **Competitively bid your large service contracts.** Large service contracts, such as Management Company, landscaping, pool maintenance, maintenance & repair, etc., should be competitively bid every couple of years. Other areas to which Boards should pay close attention to include: mortgage rates and lines of equity/credit; insurance coverage/premiums; fuel and utilities; laundry facilities providers; pest control; and elevator, boiler, and other mechanical component maintenance contracts.

– **Benchmark your suppliers.** The first thing you should do is to completely understand your current costs and what you are paying for. As with all industries, the suppliers, contractors, and service providers within the condo and homeowner industry demonstrate a wide spectrum of fees and prices. So it pays to solicit comparative bids from several of those companies qualified to do the work or to provide the service in question. To have any chance of negotiating favorable arrangements with your suppliers, you must have knowledge of the prevailing market prices and practices. Establish a market intelligence gathering system and update that system at regular intervals. Find out if there are any new technologies or suppliers that can immediately reduce your costs and administrative time. Generally, buyers are severely disadvantaged because the supplier has superior knowledge and, not surprisingly, chooses not to divulge it. Track down the prevailing market prices before starting negotiations (don't rely on suppliers for this information). Compare your cost-management performance to others in your industry and region. Benchmarking will highlight areas that have the most potential for improvement and will help you to set priorities. Use this information to negotiate from a position of strength with your suppliers.

– **Prepare Bid Requests/Request for Proposals (RFP).** To prepare a RFP for some service specifications, the association may need to draw on the technical skills and knowledge of such parties as an engineer, architect or supplier. Because of the amount of effort the bidding process requires for both the association and the bidders, the process should be used only for significant projects or purchases and for on-going services such as landscaping, pool, common element cleaning (Association), trash hauling etc. The BoD should determine the minimum size of a contract that requires competitive bidding. There are essential clauses that should be part of every contract between a homeowners association and its suppliers. These key terms give the association substantial legal benefits in the event of a dispute, mediation, arbitration or lawsuit concerning non payment or a failure to properly perform contractual duties. These protections will only be assured by using a properly drafted association form of agreement supplied by the association, or negotiating with the supplier to include them in the form of a contract provided by the supplier. The following are standard provisions that should be considered for a RFP.

- **Scope of Work.** Far too many contracts have only a cursory description of the labor and materials that will be provided under the agreement. The contract should include a detailed specification of the services and materials being purchased so that the performance of the contract can be measured. In construction contracts of any significant magnitude, plans and specifications should be prepared by an architect, engineer, or in some circumstances, the construction manager. Clarifying the scope of work is a good way of confirming the parties expectations about exactly what their respective duties and rights are under the contract.

- **Type I Indemnity.** Indemnity is the concept of shifting an economic loss or responsibility from one party to another. There are many forms of indemnity. One common form is referred to as "Type 1". A Type 1 indemnity protects the association and manager from liability against any claim, liability, lawsuit, loss, damage, or expense, including attorney's fees, arising out of the contract, including personal injury, death or economic loss. The key aspect of a Type 1 indemnity is that the legal protection extends whether or not the association or manager is alleged to have contributed to the damages. It excludes only damages or injury caused by the sole negligence or willful misconduct of the indemnitee. In conjunction with the supplier's insurance, it shifts the risk of a lawsuit to the supplier.

- **Insurance.** Suppliers should be required to maintain proper levels of workers compensation insurance and comprehensive general liability insurance. The contract must require that the association be named as an additional insured on the policy and that evidence of such insurance be provided during the performance of the agreement. As liability insurance companies are prohibiting contractors from performing work for common interest developments without a special endorsement, it is important for the contract to require, and for the association to verify, that the insurance is applicable for the planned work. The endorsements under which the association is named on the contractor's policy vary in language. The association should consult with its insurance professional or attorney to assure that the association's rights under the contractor's insurance are maximized. A mere certificate of insurance is insufficient.

- **Licensure.** In some states, work on a project for which the combined value of labor, materials and all other costs on one or more contracts is more than Five Hundred Dollars ($500) is required to be performed by a licensed contractor. The contract should state the contractor's license number of the supplier and the license categories held. It is easy to verify that the contractor has the appropriate category of license and that the license is current and active at the website maintained by the Contractors State License Board. The association may be deemed to be the employer of an unlicensed contractor for purposes of workers compensation liability and certain tax filing responsibilities. The hiring of an unlicensed contractor may in some circumstances be below the standard of care required of community association directors and therefore could give rise to a claim by the corporation against the directors for any damages that result.

- **Entity Status.** The true legal name of the contracting supplier must be inserted in the contract, so that, in the event of litigation, the legally responsible party is properly identified. Also, a routine check should be made to determine whether the supplier is in good standing with the Secretary of State. Corporations or limited liability companies that are suspended cannot legally enter into contracts.

- **Warranty.** The specific terms of all labor and material warranties must be included in the contract. The agreement must state the duration and scope of the warranty. For example, the roofing contractor's warranty can protect against defective workmanship, and also for the cost of repair of damages from leaks to the building and residence interiors.

- **Retention.** Construction contracts should provide that the progress payments to the contractor are subject to retention, typically ten percent (10%) of the amount due. The retention is held until a defined date after completion of the contract, as security for the contractor's obligation to assure that all subcontractors and material suppliers have been paid. Without such payment, these "strangers" can record and enforce mechanics liens against association controlled property even if the association had no specific agreement with these subcontractors or suppliers.

- **Completion.** The contract should contain a start and completion date. Consideration should be given to a liquidated damages clause, establishing a daily penalty for late completion. In the absence of a completion date, the law imposes only a requirement of completion within a reasonable time.

- **Termination.** An association ordinarily may terminate a contract only if the contract permits that, or if the supplier materially breaches the agreement. Proving a material breach of the contract is often difficult. Therefore, to protect the association's right to terminate a contractor at any time, it is necessary to include a clause permitting termination at any time without the necessity of proving cause (a provision sometimes called termination for "owner convenience"). There are contracts where the association does not want the contractor to have the right to terminate without cause, however, so careful consideration is necessary with regard to a reciprocal right of termination. Further, even if the association has the right to terminate without cause, it may still be held responsible for payment of some portion of the contract, including "profit".

- Create a preferred supplier list. Preferred supplier lists prevent your total supplier list from getting out of control. This is the process where the association identifies potential suppliers for specified supplies, services or equipment. These suppliers' credentials (qualifications) and history are analyzed, together with the products or services they offer.

- Send out a Request for Proposals RFP) to the preferred suppliers. A (RFP) is a message sent from your association to your preferred suppliers declaring the association's need for a product or service. RFPs are a "reverse market" where customers publish their needs/requirements/specifications and suppliers can respond with their offer/price/terms. This creates an environment where the association has a direct say in the product or solution, as opposed to accepting a solution that by its very nature is advantageous to the supplier. Once suppliers are selected, collaborate with them to see what ideas they have to help you achieve greater success.

– **Negotiate the contract.** Negotiating is a key skill set needed to obtain the desired services in the most cost effective manner. Price is often perceived as a starting point for many negotiations. However a skilled negotiator, first explores the wider opportunities to improve the "value for the money" package offered by negotiating better terms and conditions such as:

- Technical support – warranties, maintenance agreements, life-cycle support
- Financial aspect – deposit, payment terms/schedule, discount, cancellation penalties etc.
- Risk management aspects – financial guarantees, insurances, warranties, service standards, etc.
- Timeframes – completion dates, delivery dates, milestone achievement, length of contract, etc.
- Performance incentives
- After all these matters have been negotiated, then it would be appropriate to negotiate the final price. Negotiations should not be a competitive sport where there is a winner and a loser. Thus, if it is treated as a competition, the negotiation process may yield short-term gains; long-term gains, however, are not a likely result. Also, treating one's counterpart as an opponent rather than as a partner in a collaborative process decreases the likelihood of reaching an agreement that contains the fundamental element of commitment.

– **Selection the preferred supplier and award the contract.** This is the process an association utilizes to procure goods and services. Processes vary significantly from the stringent to the very informal.

Essentially the association uses some type of selection criteria to eventually select the preferred supplier. Then, that supplier is notified that they have been chosen and the final details of the contract are formalized and signed.

– **Post-award administration.** Develop a scorecard for keeping track of the supplier's service, quality, delivery and pricing. Implement a monitoring program (metrics, customer complaint system) to understand the service / issues.

  ▪ Track the quality, service and price performance of your supplier.

  ▪ Communicate the results of your scorecard to the suppliers.

  ▪ Understand what is important to your suppliers and make sure they understand what is important to your company.

- **Scrutinize all other contracted services.** An association should completely understand and justify all of the services they are paying for and the amount being paid. By looking to justify every service item, an association may discover some items that are not necessary at all and others that do not need to be as large as they have been. This type of approach forces an association to examine what it wants to spend and to make certain that the return is worth it. In addition to finding ways to reduce costs, this approach may result in a decision to increase costs in a certain area, because you expect the increased costs to produce a higher return.

- **Negotiation strategy alternatives.**

  – Negotiate a "most favored nation" clause with suppliers, so that an association is guaranteed that the price they pay is no higher than other associations (or associations of similar volume) pay.

  – Confront suppliers, and re-bid the order where appropriate, when suppliers announce a price increase.

  – Buy in bulk. Consider forming an alliance with other condo associations to obtain bulk discounts.

- Give exclusive contracts when it is highly advantage. If not, consider breaking the contract down in smaller segments and awarding each piece individually. Or, award the contract to two different suppliers performing essentially the same service for different parts of the association.

- Negotiate a fixed price contract, whereby a price is fixed for a given number of years. This protects the association from annual price increases, in exchange for a commitment not to rebid the contract during that time period.

- Negotiate a contract that calls for annual decreases in price. As a supplier becomes familiar with the service being provided to the association, it is normal for them to go through an acceleration curve where it they will become more efficient at providing that service over time. As their costs decrease, it would be desirable to pass along those efficiencies to the association in the form of annual price decreases.

- For associations in severe financial difficulty, they may want to mandate an across the board supplier cost reduction program of 3 to 5% for all of the association's service providers. Any supplier unwilling to reduce their prices should be rebid and told that they would be ineligible for future business.

- Share competitor bids to encourage more favorable price and/or service.

- **Competitively source your small service projects.** For small service needs, it is not necessary to get three competitive bids along with a comprehensive contract. Likewise, it is not necessary to have a professional contractor perform small maintenance tasks or to fix every little problem.

  - **Handyman Services.** For condo or homeowner associations that can't afford a full time maintenance person, contract with a licensed, bonded and insured handyman who can perform a monthly "laundry list" of small repairs. Combine tasks to provide a full day's work.

- **Apartment Service Providers.** Another way to determine if you are getting the "best deal" from your Management Company when it comes to routing maintenance services is to contact companies who provide this type of property maintenance for apartment complexes.
- **Moonlighters.** In most buildings, the building staff moonlights as painters and general repairpersons. Talk to your staff and see if they would like to make extra money by doing some of the work that normally a professional would do. The best example of this approach is touch-up painting in halls and stairwells. Develop a closer alliance with subcontractors to perform work in the neighborhood to get small projects done quickly and cost effectively.
- **Volunteers.** You may have members who have special skills/hobbies (engineers, contractors, woodworkers, gardeners, skilled trades, etc.) who may be willing to perform small maintenance duties or projects. Do no be afraid to ask for their help. The use of volunteers is an excellent way to help keep your costs down.

- **Pick the right time of the year.** In many areas, the late fall and winter months are slow for many types of contractors. In cold climates, for instance, painters see their workload drop dramatically because the weather prevents them from painting exteriors. Plumbers and electricians are often dependent on spring and summer construction for their jobs, so their workload drops off as well. If you have a costly project in mind -- such as painting the interior common space, installing a new laundry room, or putting up emergency lighting throughout your building -- consider getting bids in the fall and having the work done in the winter. You might save a significant amount of money. When you ask for the bid, be upfront. Tell the contractor, you're collecting bids from several others. Also, explain that you're thinking of having the project done during the late autumn or early winter because you want a good price. Also, make it clear that you not only want a good price, you want a quality job.

- **Take Preventive Measures when repairing or replacing the capital assets of the association.** Unfortunately, because of the lack of money, sometimes an association's BoD may make a short-term financial decision that will haunt them in the long term. This is particularly true for large capital replacement expenditures such as roof, siding, pool, etc. What may seem to be a good financial decision at the time may have to be "redone" at the association member's expense, due to shoddy construction techniques, no building permits, no written warranty, not dealing with a reputable firm, etc. To help prevent that, it is recommended that the following steps be taken for any large capital repair or replacement:

    – Based on a professional analysis, the BoD agrees that the capital asset needs to be repaired or replaced and the necessary funds will be provided.

    – The BoD or a designated representative (ad hoc committee, Management Company, volunteer, etc) prepares a bid package (RFP) and obtains at least three written competitive proposals/bids from professional contractors.

    – The BoD or designated representative checks and documents the references of all bidders, including work done on similar projects.

    – The BoD calls the owners to an informational meeting to report the results of the professional evaluation, to present the bids and results of checking the references and jobs done by the three bidders, and to discuss the financial impact of the repair or replacement.

    – Taking into account the opinions of the owners, the BoD awards the contract to the preferred supplier or contractor. They should negotiate any final details of the contract and both parties should sign the RFP document that includes the standard terms and conditions for the association, including indemnification, warranty, insurance, and liability clauses.

— Before any work is started, the BoD should obtain a copy of the supplier's performance bond and insurance policy along with any required licenses or permits.

When the above steps are not taken by the Board in making decisions, the fiduciary responsibility of making proper financial decisions may come under question. The declaration and bylaws of most condo or homeowner associations specifically mandate that the BoD is not fulfilling its fiduciary responsibility if the capital assets of the association are not properly maintained or finances are used poorly.

Appendix P – Litigation & Legal Fees

Background:

Condo and homeowner associations are always looking for ways to save money and one prime area where some cost-cutting opportunities might be found is in their legal expenses. This could come in the form of reduced attorney fees or unfavorable litigation expenses. Legal fees may be a necessary association expense, but, many associations pay more than they should. Perhaps your association has been using a reliable law firm for several years but you're troubled by the size of the bills. Or maybe you're looking for an attorney to provide legal services to your association. In either situation, you may be able to save a great in legal fees without compromising the quality of the services you receive. One of the most important, yet neglected, areas where associations can reduce legal exposure and expense, is through preventive actions that reduce their risk. Prevention is really better than cure – and it is cheaper too!

Data and Pertinent Information:

- Being sued or finding yourself in a position where you have no real choice but to sue should almost always be avoided. However, litigation may be necessary and should even sometimes be employed to further broad strategic association objectives.
- By spending a little now, you may be able to save a lot later. Granted, most condo or homeowner associations operate with tight financial resources and may be reluctant to spend money on legal matters. But don't be afraid to invest "before the fact" in legal protections and other measures that may prevent far more costly lawsuits and attorney fees further down the road.

- Don't give in to the impulse to fight for the last dollar because "a matter of principle" is involved. Usually, it's better to compromise a conflict than to fight it through trial. You may even be able to settle some minor matters yourself without an attorney's help.

- Perhaps the biggest factor in terms of keeping legal fees under control is to know when, and when not, to contact your attorney. Don't procrastinate too long, but don't be too quick to call your attorney. Sometimes Boards decide on their own that they can handle a particular matter, which they know has legal ramifications, but they don't want to contact the attorney because they know that costs them money. Then, they may find that it's costing them more money to get out of the problem than it would have if they had just called consulted with an attorney in the first place. One area that needs particular attention is contracts with vendors like electricians, roofers and carpenters.

- There are several ways to resolve legal disputes or for preventing them from becoming legal disputes, which are summarized below:
  - **Face-to-face.** If the issue is between two owners, encourage them to talk to each other to find a resolution. But, don't be surprised if they are reluctant to do this. As a BoD, you should try to avoid getting in the middle of these disputes or taking sides, as it typically is a no-win situation. Encourage discussion and offer options, but try to get them to resolve their own problem. If the issue is between the BoD and a association member, you might try the same approach, if you haven't already done so.
  - **Negotiation/Compromise.** Negotiation is the process of offer and counter offer until agreement is reached. Compromise is usually involved with one or both parties with the objective of finding a win-win solution.
  - **Mediation.** Mediation can be voluntary or it may be required by statute, court rule or CC&Rs. It is a process used for parties who have a conflict that they have been unable to resolve. Trained

mediators meet with the parties to discuss their concern and the cause of the dispute. They assist the parties in reaching a solution that will work for them and end the dispute. The mediator(s) write down the specifics of the agreement. This agreement is binding and enforceable by those who sign it unless otherwise stated in the agreement. It is relatively inexpensive and the parties usually split the mediator's fees.

   – **Arbitration**. Arbitration may be voluntary or "required" due to provisions in an agreement or governing documents. It is similar to traditional litigation and an arbitrator decides the case, just like a judge would do. The decision is typically "binding," but may not be if an association CC&Rs or Statures allow court action after arbitration if a party is unhappy. It is expensive.

   – **Litigation**. The results are binding on both parties and the proceedings are open to the public. This can be a very expensive proposition due to attorney fees and court costs.

• One particularly troublesome issue is owner bankruptcy. The general sequence of events is that they don't pay their mortgage or maintenance for six or eight months. Then they file for bankruptcy, which gives them another three or four months. And with the bankruptcy laws being so sophisticated, if you don't react or hire somebody who knows what they're doing, you can expect a long and drawn out process that in the end may get you nothing except attorney expenses to pay.

Recommendations/Alternatives to Be Considered:

• **Be proactive and not reactive.** The fact is most lawsuits are preventable if a BoD proactively manages trouble. Never stick your head in the sand regarding association member complaints and do not ignore them. Far too many small problems fester into a lawsuit simply because someone didn't pay sufficient attention to dealing with them when they were minor. You should never let a lawsuit take you by surprise. One of the most effective ways to prevent a lawsuit is to acknowledge the possibility of one — and, from there, to take every possible proactive step to prevent a lawsuit. Identify those elements and functions of your association's business that are most critical, and pinpoint volatile items within those areas. Then, work out planned responses so that problems are dealt with effectively and as a matter of course.

- **Reduce your risks.** Manage your risks wisely. Rely on common sense. If it looks dangerous it probably is. Address it now and don't wait for the next BoD meeting that might be several months down the road. As a Board member you have a responsibility to do that and you don't want to wait until a claim occurs because these claims one way or another are going to cost you money. The BoD must evaluate exactly what their liabilities are and take measures to remedy them. Areas to examine include:

  - **Security.** Ensuring that all doors are locked at all times, particularly out of the way basement doors and rear entries, lowers liability and increases the safety of the residents. Install security systems in common areas, basements and laundry rooms.

  - **Preventative maintenance items.** Practice good maintenance and provide a save environment - no wet floors or trip/fall hazards, clear and well-lit stairwells, fixing a staircase that needs a banister, adhering to building codes, etc. Consider anything that might potentially cause unwarranted exposure from such things as; fire, mold contamination, and other unforeseen events. Beware of water damage - keep roofs, terraces, pipes and foundations in good repair.

  - **Workers compensation.** Make sure to provide a safe working atmosphere for any of your employees and don't allow them to do a job that they're not trained for. It is important that you obtain insurance for all of the contractors that will be working at your property. Every contractor that sets foot on your premises should provide a certificate of insurance.

— **Standard contract forms.** Periodically reviewing the association's standard contract forms to ensure they incorporate recent changes in law and include provisions that are consistent with the association's current risk profile.

— **Contract management.** Associations enter into all sorts of contracts for many types of projects ranging from landscaping to pool maintenance and repair, to name a few. In order to protect the association and its investment, the association should ensure that it has an effective contract with the service provider. A contract will clarify the scope of work the contractor will perform, giving the association a way to measure the quality of service provided. All contracts should be in writing, incorporating all the material terms and conditions of the transaction, and contemplate how the parties will handle events that may occur during the performance of the contract. Sad to say, but the day when a businessperson's handshake was good enough, is not enough to protect an association's interests in current times. Completion time frames, costs, liabilities and other relevant details are often glossed over or ignored if the contract isn't written out. Make sure the agreement specifies how disputes will be resolved, including those that may crop up during the life of the agreement. For example, many contracts specify that the parties agree to arbitration, mediation or some other form of dispute resolution short of handling it in the court system. Those and other options can often prove invaluable in avoiding a lengthy and expensive legal battle.

— **Attorney review.** Depending on the nature of a contract, its complexity, or cost, it may be advisable and prudent to have the association attorney review a contract agreement that is about to be signed. Getting everything down on paper is only one protective element. But even well-intentioned written contracts can be troublesome if they contain some loophole or other issue that the other party can exploit. So, make sure that your attorney appropriately reviews anything contractually important you plan on signing.

- Insurance. BoD's can sometimes avoid legal fees by carrying adequate insurance coverage. A standard liability policy in tandem with directors' and officers' coverage will provide a legal defense for a condo or homeowner association or BoD member named as a defendant in a lawsuit. More often than not, however, litigation expenses are not covered by insurance because it is usually the association that initiates the suit.

- **Standardize routine legal tasks.** Analyze routine legal tasks performed by outside counsel and determine whether the tasks can be performed without — or with minimal — counsel involvement. Procedures or "how to" guides can be implemented by the association to allow support staff to complete routine tasks that are otherwise performed by legal professionals. Routine tasks that can be internalized are numerous, and could include preparation of standard contracts, filing of mechanics' liens, and preparation of corporate minutes, routine resolutions and consents.

- **Appropriately use your Management Company.** An association can also save money through judicious use of its legal talent. The last thing you want to do is to turn your attorney into a "junior Managing Agent." Make sure that you are fully utilizing your Management Company to handle routine legal issues that they are capable of handling (or who can become capable of handling.) Many phone calls or other routine legal issues could probably be resolved by the Managing Agent who is already receiving compensation.

- **Settle cases rather than litigate.** Don't give in to the impulse to fight for the last dollar because "a matter of principle" is involved. You may have to swallow your pride on occasion. Consider compromise and settlement — even if you know you did nothing wrong, it's cheaper than going to court. Even if you're in the right, offering a discount, compromising a bill or even offering an apology will almost always trump the eventual cost of a lawsuit. You may even be able to settle some minor matters yourself without the attorney's help. Identify where you are willing to compromise and where you are not. Look for win-win situations, even it means that you don't get exactly what you want. Make sure you completely understand the issue at hand and try to identify alternative ways to resolve the problem, rather than limiting yourselves to either your or the other party's recommended solution. Managing litigation expenses by aggressively limiting unnecessary discovery and performing cost benefit analyses to decide if settlement or alternate dispute resolution is a better option.

- **Arbitrate or mediate.** BoD's can also avoid expensive litigation by using arbitration or mediation. An arbitrator's decision is typically binding on the parties. Condo or homeowner associations that want to force unit owners to accept binding arbitration may have to amend their bylaws. This may not be necessary if both sides agree to arbitration. Mediation is nonbinding, with voluntary reconciliation as its goal. It is always available and frequently successful.

- **Attorney on retainer.** Your association may find it advantageous to have an attorney on a retainer. Some attorneys say paying your attorney a set annual fee is one way to keep costs under control. Retainers can cover services like writing letters, reading contracts, telephone calls and attending annual meetings, as well as a limited number of other Board meetings. They will charge a lower hourly rate as opposed to those who are working on a case-to-case basis. If you guarantee a minimum number of hours of work during the year, a $200 an hour attorney may be willing to work for $175 an hour. BoD's who want a attorney permanently on call should consider asking the attorney to assign a less expensive associate to more routine matters or to work on retainer rather than an hourly basis. An hour here and an hour there eventually turns into big money.

- **Competitive bid.** BoD's should put their legal services out to competitive bid, just like any other of its major service contracts. Conducting a request for proposal process will require law firms to compete for business and will be more likely to provide lower rates, which also may include creative fee proposals. With today's communications technologies that are available, you do not have to restrict your search to local firms to minimize travel time. Face-to-face meetings are not needed (except for maybe the first contracting meeting) and virtually everything can be handled electronically or over the phone. Now, you can go after the attorney that gives you the best quality and lowest cost performance.

- **Get the right attorney for the job.** When litigation is unavoidable, make sure you get the attorney whose practice focuses on the narrow area of law in which you need assistance. (This almost always means you need more than one law firm doing your legal work, by the way.) You don't want to be paying for on-the-job training. If you have a foreclosure problem, hire an expert in foreclosures. If you have an eviction situation, hire an expert in landlord-tenant law.

- **Discuss the billing arrangement at the start.** Don't be shy about bringing up the billing arrangements early on in the attorney selection process. Remember, attorneys are in typically in business for themselves and are free to set their own fees. It's often appropriate for you to negotiate regarding these charges. The best time to discuss fees is at the beginning of a new legal matter. You should ask if any incentives are available, such as the initial call or meeting. It is in your best interest to get an estimate of your legal costs that you are likely to encounter. Explore alternative fee arrangements. It almost always makes sense to at least discuss with your attorney billing arrangements other than straight hourly fees. Perhaps you'll both benefit from a fixed fee arrangement.

- **Manage your legal costs.** There are also some simple, common-sense steps that BoD's can take to keep legal costs down.

  - **Saving attorney time is saving money.** Since you are typically paying for an attorney's time, you should do everything possible to minimize the amount of time required on their part including:

    - **Eliminate all attorney travel time.** In today's electronic age, it is no longer necessary to incur this expense. Arrange for meetings in your attorney's office, over the phone, or through e-mail. It is wasteful to pay for your attorney's travel time.

    - **Prepare for attorney meetings.** List all your concerns in priority order and weed out those topics that are not necessary for the meeting. It is surprising how many topics can be covered in an hour. Have all your information ready and do not hesitate to insist that everyone stick to the point.

    - **Eliminate multiple contacts between the BoD and the attorney.** Assign one BoD member (and maybe a second as a backup) to be the BoD liaison with the attorney. You can eliminate the problem of having the attorney give the same answer to several BoD members—and billing for each individual communication.

  - **Minimize the attorney time spent at a BoD meeting.** Do not have an attorney present if there is no need for one. Look for ways to handle an issue rather than handling it in a BoD meeting with the presence of an attorney. If there's just one item on an agenda that requires the attorney's input, make it the first thing you cover in the meeting. Better yet, eliminate travel and wait time costs by connecting the attorney through a conference call/speaker phone when their input is needed. You may want to e-mail your minutes to your attorney as a preventive matter. Spending maybe 10 or 15 minutes looking at the e-mail and respond to it is a lot cheaper than having an attorney sit through a multiple hour BoD meeting.

– Check that Bill. You should always review your invoice for billing errors. Also, you press your attorney for an estimate/guess-timate for the cost of a service. Then the attorney will have to justify any actual costs that are significantly different.

Appendix Q – Preventative Maintenance

Background:

In a falling real estate market, a special effort must often be made to preserve values by performing needed maintenance and repairs instead of putting them off. A BoD would be wise to put themselves into the perspective of would-be buyers and take a look at what can be done to improve curb appeal. Weedy common plantings, dead trees and shrubs, peeling paint, cupping shingles, and crumbling pavement all evidence a failure by the Association to properly maintain the project and can have a negative impact on potential sales that may in turn trap a seller and turn him or her into a delinquent co-owner.

Preventive Maintenance (PM) is always the least costly and most effective form of maintenance. It will ensure that the association's assets are always maintained at the optimum level of condition. PM is used to preserve buildings, equipment and physical grounds through regular inspections and performance of certain maintenance tasks. PM is particularly important in condo or homeowner associations due to the higher level of use and potential risk to owners and visitor safety if problems should occur due to lack of maintenance.

PM does not stop the aging and deterioration of association assets, but it is the most effective method available to ensure that all components achieve the maximum life and performance cycle that can be expected. If properly implemented a PM will, in many cases, prolong the useful life of components beyond the typical life spans that are assumed.

Preventive maintenance has proven to be more popular in principle than in practice over the years even when a range of solid arguments are presented, including:

- The equipment will perform better.
- Equipment/asset life will be extended.
- Repair costs will decrease.
- Downtime will be reduced.
- Owner satisfaction will increase.

Avoiding "emergency" repairs, which could have been predicted, is one of your biggest money savers. Emergency repairs almost always cost more than planned repairs and may not be competitively bid due to time constraints.

Data and Pertinent Information:

- The strength of any preventive maintenance program relies on a consistent inspection program. Structures, landscaping, and amenities need to be consistently observed to detect minor concerns before they become major problems. A good PM program involves a consistent investment of time, effort, and resources that can help postpone or prevent many unnecessary repair and replacement costs. This is especially important as buildings, facilities, and landscaping naturally age and accumulates everyday wear and tear. A well-planned and implemented PM program can maximize the normal life of structural, landscape, and other assets.
- If a preventive maintenance program is implemented, an association can not only help protect itself from unscheduled special assessments, but will enhance the unit values as well. The purpose of preventive maintenance is to spend some money now to save a lot later.
- Preventive maintenance is also a very important element of an association's reserve funding strategy. If the components on the reserve schedule are not properly maintained, they will not attain their full useful life. Consequently, the components will need to be replaced

earlier and the replacement cost will need to be collected over a shorter period of time. This could result in possible special assessments. The BoD should develop a written preventative maintenance policy to set a standard and procedure for maintaining common components.

- For those condo or homeowner associations looking at leaner budgets ahead, a BoD may:
  - Hold off on any proposed capital spending until the cash flow of the association improves. Deferring spending on unnecessary or "luxury" maintenance costs, such as upgrading a lobby or renovating a basement, until a BoD can reasonably afford these items can save a considerable amount of money.
  - Initiating minor improvements on existing building systems is also more feasible than installing new equipment.
  - Doing an extra round of preventive maintenance instead of a scheduled replacement (i.e. patch and seal coating for asphalt roads and pushing back scheduled resurfacing). Don't just skip everything, only those that waiting a year or two won't do any harm or look bad.
- One of the areas often confusing to a unit owner (or association for that matter) is who has maintenance, repair or replacement responsibility for a specific element of building and/or common area items? A Maintenance Responsibility Matrix can be an extremely helpful tool in clarifying these responsibilities.

Recommendations/Alternatives to Be Considered:

- **Preventative maintenance policy.** The BoD first needs go on record that it is committed philosophically to preventative maintenance. A PM policy sets a standard and procedure for maintaining common components. This policy allows the BoD to make consistent choices and brings structure and continuity to maintenance decisions. It should also be integral component of an associations Reserve funding strategy. Shown below is an example of a PM policy.

ABC Condominium Association
Preventative Maintenance Policy

Preventative maintenance of common elements, as may be authorized by the Board of Directors, shall be done in accordance with the following policy:

A) The Board is committed philosophically to preventative maintenance (PM) as a mechanism to prolong useful life of common area components and to minimize costs. The purpose of preventive maintenance is to spend some money now to save a lot later.

B) All common elements will be inspected on an annual basis to determine if any PM or repairs may be necessary.

C) The Maintenance & Repair Committee will develop a maintenance plan for each common element requiring attention assuring that "professional" lasting repairs are made and that "band-aid" remedies are avoided.

D) The association's annual budget should be built around the maintenance program recommendations

---

- **Maintenance & Responsibility Matrix.** The BoD should develop a Maintenance & Responsibility Matrix that defines whether the association or unit owner is responsible for the maintenance/repair/replacement of specific components. This document is to assist the owners in understanding the association's role and responsibility in the care of the common property. It also provides the association with a list of responsibilities that it can then use to build its preventative maintenance program. A sample Maintenance & Responsibility Matrix is provided.

- **Physical Property Inspection.** Physically inspect the components on the scheduled basis and perform the necessary maintenance and/or repair. Many associations have never taken the time to walk around the property on a "maintenance inspection" and those that do often do not possess the proper skills. Choose the people carefully that will perform this duty. When needed, include reputable, licensed and qualified contractors, engineer or architectural consultants, or certified building inspectors. These people have a trained eye which will pick up potential problems that laymen would miss. Although they may charge for their time, they will save money in the long run.

- **Preventative Maintenance schedule.** Identify what items need to be included in your preventative maintenance program and define in writing the inspection procedures and recommended maintenance. To determine what needs to be done to each item to maintain it, talk to your suppliers and subcontractors who sold and installed each item. Service booklets with maintenance schedules and requirements are typically supplied with appliances and equipment. Shown below is a sample list of common items to include in your program and what should be done for each. Since each property is different, this is not a complete list. For example, a high-rise building will probably have elevators, fire sprinklers, and a central HVAC with a chiller tower. By doing a complete walk through of the property, you can create a list of everything that will be included in the program.

(Sample)
Preventative Maintenance Plan

Description	Inspection Procedure	Freq.
Water Heater	Inspect, drain and descale.	Annual
Carpet	Professionally clean common area carpet at least once a year to prolong its life.	Annual
Rain gutters & downspouts	Inspect for secure fastening. Clean prior to winter or rainy season; clean out underground drains as needed.	Annual
Roofs and Flashing	Inspect and clean annually prior to winter or rainy season; look for obvious problems like missing shingles, breaks in the membrane; contract with a roofing contractor to perform this function automatically prior to winter.	Annual
Storm Drains	Inspect and clean.	Semi-annual
HVAC	Clean coils, change filters, oil motors	Quarterly
Photocells	Inspect, test and clean	Quarterly
Exterior of buildings	Inspect for wood rot, loose or damaged trim, paint deterioration and loose or damaged siding.	Quarterly

Swimming Pool	Inspect filters and pumps, oil and adjust.	Quarterly
Lawn Sprinklers	Inspect, test, replace heads, and reset timers.	Weekly
Parking Lot	Inspect for cracks and potholes.	Weekly
Exterior, Common Area and Signage Lighting	Inspect and adjust timers or photocells.	Weekly
Fire Extinguishers	Inspect and recharge.	Anytime
Smoke Alarms	Inspect and test battery.	Anytime
Exterior Doors	Inspect weather stripping, thresholds, hinges, door closers and locks.	Anytime
Balcony and Stairwell Railings	Inspect for secure fastening.	Anytime

- The following are other candidates for an association's PM program.

  - FOUNDATIONS, BASEMENTS, and YARDS
    - Water that strikes the house or drips down from the roof should drain away from the foundation walls. The gutter and downspout system should keep water from pooling around the foundation where it can create a moisture problem. Be sure gutters and downspouts are kept open and in good repair. The main drainage swales, culverts, basins and pipes should be periodically checked, and repaired as needed.
    - Trim shrubs and bushes away from the foundation walls. Clearance space should be at least one foot. Prune trees every 3-5 years to eliminate deadwood, enhance shaping and identify treatable diseases and pests.
    - Check masonry foundation walls for cracks or weakened, crumbling mortar.
    - Examine main support beams, support columns, and floor joists for evidence of bowing or warping.

- Check wood structural members, such as joists, beams, and columns, with a screwdriver or pocket knife to be sure wood is solid and free from decay.
- Check the inside and outside of all foundation walls and piers for termite tubes and damage. You may choose to have an insect-control company to do this each year.
- Check that the crawl space vapor barrier is in good condition and placed correctly.
- Examine the inside of basement walls for dampness or water stains indicating seepage or a leak.
- In most areas, water lines and outside faucets need some freeze protection or winter drainage.
- Clean leaves and debris from around an outside heating/air conditioning condenser and trim back shrubs that may block air movement around the house.
- Doorways, below grade window wells, and storm drains should be cleaned of debris or leaves.
- Power sweep/vacuum parking surfaces.
- Inspect/maintain/repair drains, curbs, and gutters.
- Remove dirt, litter, and debris from the common property concrete surfaces.
- Driveways and walks should be checked for cracks, breaks, or erosion that may damage them. If asphalt surfaces need repairing, be certain you have the equipment and skill to do a lasting repair job. Otherwise, choose a reputable contractor. Unrepaired cracks in concrete can lead to further damage.
- Check concrete for deficiencies which cause structural problems or tripping hazards, which should be replaced for safety, as well as liability prevention and aesthetic reasons

- A septic tank needs periodic attention. Learn how to check for sludge and scum accumulation in the tank, and have solids pumped out of the tank as needed.
- Fences, gates, and retaining walls should be checked for ease of operation, condition of structure, and materials. Make repairs as needed.
- Wrap any trees or shrubs susceptible to winter burn during the winter months
- Inspect the irrigation system and perform any recommended maintenance. Be sure to blow out water from irrigation lines during winter months to prevent freezing damage.
- Inspect plant material for water needs.
- Inspect/maintain/repair all turf areas for safety hazards

- EXTERIOR WALLS, WINDOWS, and DOORS
  - Check bricks or blocks for cracked mortar or loose joints.
  - Check siding for loose or missing pieces, lifting or warping, or any sign of mildew.
  - Check painted surfaces for paint failure (peeling, chipping, blistering, chalking), water damage, or mildew. Depending on the type of siding, a program of painting, replacement and/or caulking may be necessary.
  - Examine all trim for tightness of fit, damage, or decay.
  - Check the condition of caulking where two different materials meet, such as where wood siding joins the foundation wall, at inside corners, and where window and door trim meets the siding.
  - Check the windows for cracked or broken glass, loose putty around the glass panes, holes in screens, and evidence of moisture between pane and storm windows.

- Check that windows and doors close properly. Examine all hardware on windows and doors, and lubricate moving parts.
- Check weather-stripping on windows and doors for damage and tightness of fit.
- Make sure that all window and door locks work properly. Each exterior door should have a one-inch deadbolt lock for safety.

– ROOF

- Trim back tree branches that scrape against or overhang the roof. Keep branches away from chimney to avoid fire hazard and allow proper draft for safe and efficient chimney operation.
- Check for curled, damaged, loose, or missing shingles.
- Check the lower edge of roof sheathing for water damage.
- Examine all roof flashing and the flashing around chimneys, vent stacks, roof edges, dormers, and skylights.
- Make sure that the chimney cover (cap) is in good condition, and that it is tall enough to prevent creosote build-up.
- Check vents and louvers for free air movement. Clean screens and remove bird nests, spiders, insects, and dust.
- If there are wind turbines on the roof, check ball bearings. Clear gable vents of bird's nests and other obstructions.
- Check for damaged gutters, downspouts, hangers, and strainers. If needed, clean out gutters and downspouts. Make sure they are free from leaks and rust.
- Check the condition of paint on gutters.
- Examine and television antenna guy wires and support straps or satellite dish mountings.

– INTERIOR SURFACES

- Check all ceilings and walls for cracks, loose or failing plaster, signs of leaks or stains, dirt, and finish damage.
- Check for cracks where ceilings join walls and where moldings attach to ceilings and walls.
- Check for odor or visible evidence of mildew or mold.
- Examine all joints in ceramic tiles and laminated plastics for adequate caulking. Have any of the tiles cracked or become discolored?
- Check all floors for wear and damage. Are the floors level, bowed, or do they squeak when you walk on them? Particularly check where one type of flooring material meets another, such as where carpet or wood joins tile.
- Check stairs for loose treads, handrails, or carpeting, and repair as needed.
- Elevators: Do an annual inspection of the shaft, pit and equipment room with the contractor to ensure that proper maintenance is being performed.

– ELECTRICAL SYSTEMS and FIXTURES

- Check for exposed wires and signs of wear in the service box.
- If you have a fuse that blows often or a circuit breaker that trips frequently, call an electrician to determine the cause and make the repair. Mark each circuit so that you will know what outlets or appliances are included on each.
- Check places where wiring is exposed, such as in the attic. Look for exposed wires and wires with cracked insulation. Replace those in poor condition.

– HEATING and COOLING SYSTEMS

- Have heating and cooling systems checked by a qualified serviceperson once a year or according to the manufacturer's warranty and service recommendations.

- Clean or replace filters. Check your owner's manual for recommended procedures.
- Clean dirt and dust from around furnaces, air grills, and ducts.
- Regularly clean out fireplace ash pit.
- Check the attic to be sure that insulation or other material is not blocking free air flow through soffit vents, gable vents, or other attic vents.

– PLUMBING SYSTEMS

- Is the water pressure adequate? Do all the drains run freely?
- In a basement or crawl space house, pull back floor insulation to check for leaks and wood damage around water supply pipes, drains, and water closet.
- Check the pressure relief valve on the water heater. Open it to see that it is working. Check for signs of leaking or rusting. Some manufacturers recommend that a small amount of water be drained periodically from the tank.

• Reminder System. Choose your reminder system. This can range from automatic pop-up reminders built into software, to a manual calendar with recurring tasks noted. The ideal system is easy to update, can handle tasks scheduled for two or three years from now, and reliably prevents items from falling through the cracks. Update your PM schedule regularly. Be aware of events such as asset purchase or contract renewal that should trigger a review and update of your preventive maintenance template. An annual calendar of activities should serve as a "tickler" system so to the BoD, Management Company, staff, and even residents, to let them know exactly what is being done, and when, to keep the property functioning optimally. Such a PM program will go a long way in reducing capital expenditures and engendering a sense of confidence among residents by demonstrating to them how their maintenance or common charges payments are being used for the benefit of the property.

- Allocate the Funds. The best maintenance plan in the world is useless if not properly funded. Since money comes from the operating budget and increasing the maintenance budget is not popular, it is critical to have the plan that justifies the budget. Build the budget around the maintenance program, not vice versa.

Appendix R – Reserve Fund

Background:

Every condominium association should have an up-to-date "Reserve Study" to help it determine how and when to repair/replace major common area components (such as roofs or pavement) over the long term. Healthy reserves are critical to a financially healthy association because:

- Buyers examine the Reserves before buying
- Lenders examine the Reserves before approving a loan
- The BoD has a fiduciary responsibility to protect the association from financial hardship
- It shares the costs of maintaining the property by all owners, now and in the future
- It provides a predictable, manageable, contribution plan
- It enhances resale values
- It helps avoids large special assessments, perhaps unexpectedly

The reserve study provides the foundation for a BoD to then develop its funding strategy, which includes the contribution rate that is taken from current association fees. Providing the proper balance between current and future needs is not an exact science and the association BoD must make several decisions regarding reserve funding including the following:

- What physical assets should be covered by the reserve plan?
  - Common areas
  - Cost threshold
  - Predictable life limit
  - Current useful
- How much reserves are enough?
- Which funding principles should be used?

- What funding goal should be established?
- Which funding strategy should be followed?

But, as you can see, there are a number of variables which come into play when funding a reserve plan and in many cases; the BoD makes a judgment call on how much is enough. On one hand, they must guard against reserve "over-funding", which penalizes current members. Having too much in reserves can be just as harming to an association and unit values, as having too little. On the other hand, they must guard against reserve "under-funding", which penalizes future members who can be faced with a special assessment. In the end, they must establish reasonable reserves and contributions rates that treat both current and future homeowners as fairly as possible.

The large number of variables which make it difficult to develop a reserve strategy also provides opportunity for refinement and a better utilization of scarce association funds. This is why a reserve funding strategy should be reviewed on a regular basis to determine if it is best serving its member's needs. Current economic conditions may dictate that a different strategy be temporarily used until financial health returns. There are several cost cutting options that are always available to a BoD including; funding goals, contribution rates, and ways to extend component useful life.

Obviously, associations with a strong reserve position will have much more options at their disposal than ones with weak positions. It should be emphasized that any cost cutting measures used for changing the reserve funding strategy must be very cautiously approached.

Data and Pertinent Information:

- An association's Fully Funded Balance (FFB) is the Reserve balance that is in direct proportion to the fraction of life "used up" of the current repair or replacement cost. This benchmark balance represents the value of the deterioration of the Reserve components. This number is calculated for each component, and then summed together for an association total. Reserve fund size is measured by Percent Funded (PF), which is the actual Reserve Balance (RB) divided by the association's calculated Fully Funded Balance, expressed as a percentage Percent Funded (PF) (PF=RB/FFB) . Percent Funded is of particular importance, for it provides a general indication of reserve strength.

- The following industry guidelines have often been used to interpret this Percent Funded strength indicator in terms of risk associated with the availability of reserves to fund future expenditures. Special assessments and deferred maintenance are common when the percent funded is weak (below 30%). While the 100% point is Ideal, a Reserve fund above the 70% level should be considered "strong" because cash flow problems are rare.

Percent Funded	Level of Risk
70% and above	LOW
31% to 69%	MODERATE
30% and below	HIGH

- Lester Giese, the author of The 99 Best Residential & Recreational Communities in America, recommends the following formula: If the complex is one to 10 years old, the reserve fund should have 10% of the cost of replaceable items (roofs, roads, tennis courts, etc.). Between 10 and 20 years old, the repair fund should be at 25% to 30%. At 20 years, that amount should be 50% or above.

- Reserve funding requirements for a condo or homeowner association are established either by law or governing documents and can range from 10% to 100% fully funded.

- If delinquency problems have plagued a condo or homeowner association for several years, the reserve fund may have to be tapped if cash flow dips dangerously low. However, borrowing from your reserve accounts is like borrowing from your retirement investment accounts – it is not a good idea and should not be done unless (1) you are experiencing extreme financial conditions; (2) you follow the legal requirements, and (3) you have a plan to pay it back. Having said that, tapping your reserve account may be your only option to remain solvent, prevent you from pricing yourselves out of the market, or for preventing more delinquencies and foreclosures.

- Reserve component life expectancy can vary due to use, weather, workmanship, etc. As items get close to the projected end of their useful life, closer monitoring is warranted. There may be alternatives available to extent the useful life, thus making funds available for other uses

- Community associations have several funding schedule options, including periodic assessments over the life of the assets, special assessments at the time of the actual replacement, borrowing funds when needed, a combination of the above.

Recommendations/Alternatives to Be Considered:

- **Refresh latest reserve study**. In order to examine areas of opportunity, you must first verify that your latest reserve study is up to date and can be used as an accurate health assessment of your long-term capital assets. You should re-verify your original assumptions on such things as useful life, predicted life expectancy, inflation rate, rate of returns on investments, etc. Determine if the life expectancy can be extended through a preventative maintenance program or if there are any other areas where the life can be further extended. Divert any excess funds gained to other priorities.

- **Re-examine your funding goal.** Most condo or homeowner associations have latitude to determine what goal it will use for funding its reserve fund, subject to governing documents and law. Although most reserve fund professionals will recommend a fully funded methodology, a BoD may select one of several more attractive funding methods.

  - **"Full Funding"** is when the association has the goal of becoming 100% fully funded where the reserve cash equals the Fully Funded Balance. If you association has adopted a fully-funded goal, it has considerable latitude to use other methods of funding goals. Ironically, those that have chosen a full funding goal are probably the least likely to need cost-savings adjustment. But even then, unforeseen conditions may force it to take drastic actions.

  - **"Threshold Funding"** option is different in that the association selects a target between 0% and 100% funded, higher than 100% funded, or a particular Reserve cash balance. Associations choosing Threshold Funding select this option to customize their risk exposure.

  - **"Baseline Funding"** is when there is a goal of simply having sufficient cash for all future years. The drawback with this risky method is that there is little or no "margin for error". Expenses that are higher than budgeted or projects that occur earlier than planned will often cause special assessments.

  - **"Statutory Funding"**, where an association sets aside a specific minimum amount of reserves as required by law (i.e. - 10% of an associations' annual budget).

Since a 70% fully funded rate is still considered to be a strong position for a reserve fund, a BoD could lower its goal, with the understanding that it would have to levy an assessment in future to make up the difference. The same principle could be applied to rates between 31% and 69% indicating a moderate strength. Since it is so difficult to build up reserve funds, you will not want to use this strategy unless it is absolutely necessary. A more moderate approach may be to temporarily adjust funding goals until an association can get over its financial hump and then revert back the original funding strategy.

Appendix S – Property Taxes

Background:

For condo and homeowner association BoD's, the tax certiorari proceeding is a real opportunity to reduce real estate taxes for their buildings and for their unit owners. Real estate tax certiorari is the legal process by which a property owner can challenge the real estate tax assessment on a given property in attempt to reduce the property's assessment and real estate taxes.

The property tax is the single largest source of revenue for local governments. Each governmental unit with taxing authority has its own laws, rules and procedures for levying and collecting taxes. They make value judgments about the use of land and use different taxing formulas for businesses, homes, farms, and property deemed exempt (religious, educational, governmental, etc.).

Determining the value of property tax to be assessed is not an exact science as there are many inexact characteristics that make a property unique. The qualifications of the may also assessor affect the assessment. While most districts employ the services of a professional, some may not be a professional in the field of property assessment. Since tax assessors' offices are notoriously understaffed, many rely on software or even outside companies to figure out your bill. Even when an assessor visits, s/he may just look at your property from the sidewalk or from their car.

Most taxation units recognize the potential for error in the property tax system and have developed appeals procedures that any citizen can use. However, many will not appeal for the following reasons:

- You can't fight city hall

- The procedure requires special expertise
- An appeal will be costly and/or time consuming
- The assessor and/or elected officials will retaliate

In general, none of the above statements are true, although one may find isolated exceptions. While the system can be complex, the average person can acquire an understanding of it and can take steps to make sure that their property tax is fair and equitable. For larger condo or homeowner associations, a person specializing in this field can be used.

The immediate and long-term tax relief benefits which may result from an appeal are obvious. It is therefore wise for an association to scrutinize their assessment line by line and on a regular basis.

Data and Pertinent Information:

- Although the right to appeal a tax assessment (certiorari) is clearly specified by law, few condo or homeowner associations have exercised this right. Commercial property owners pursue these tax appeals on a regular continuing basis as standard business practice.
- The owner of a unit in a condominium or homeowner association is treated much like the owner of a one-family house when it comes to paying property taxes: S/He is assessed individually and is personally responsible for the tax bill. But this doesn't mean such people have to go it alone when it comes to protesting their assessment and the level of taxes they pay in relation to other homeowners in the community. On the contrary, they have the advantage of being able to operate as a group. One advantage is the cost savings. Most tax-appeal specialists operate on a contingency-fee basis, taking a cut of the saving generated by the appeal. The percentage falls dramatically when a package of multiple units can be linked together. In most cases these tax certiorari attorneys are paid between 12 percent and 50 percent of the savings

they obtain. Since there is no penalty for filing a certiorari appeal, and since in most cases properties are under no obligation to pay professional certiorari fees unless a reduction is realized, there is nothing to lose and everything to gain by undertaking annual certiorari appeals.

- A successful real estate tax appeal in most areas of the country is based upon first establishing the market value of your property. In order to reduce your property taxes you must prove that the value of your property is less than the valuation assigned by your assessing district (according to state law in most states, the assessment is deemed to be correct, and the burden of proof, falls on the petitioner to prove otherwise). A recent legitimate arms length sale of the subject property is the best evidence. If the property was not recently purchased, or the purchase was not at arms length (as in an inter-family sale, foreclosure or other sale made under conditions of distress), an appraisal by a state certified appraiser is the next best type of evidence, which is typically used to prove value of your home throughout the process.

- Not all cities/towns adjust their assessments every year to reflect the current market. While some municipalities do revalue properties annually, others do so every five years. So if your property was last assessed during the market peak, it makes sense to consider challenging the assessment.

- When to seek a reassessment isn't an exact science. It depends on how much your property value has declined, and on what sort of dollar gain you'll likely get in your tax bill.

Recommendations/Alternatives to Be Considered:

There are several ways to challenge your property taxes.

- **Tax appeal specialist.** Hire a tax-appeal specialist, who operates on a contingency-fee basis, to appeal the taxes of similar units within condominium or homeowner association.

- **Be a "quick follower".** If unit owner appeals their property tax (either individually or through a lawyer or tax specialist) basis, and is successful at getting their taxes reduced, obtain the information used and apply it to you unit, if it is similar.

- **Owner appeal.** If you have the time and interest, you can personally appeal your property taxes, when you are notified of the time period in which you can appeal. Shown below are the typical steps you should follow:

- **Know your taxing unit's assessment methodology.** There's wide variation in how taxing units assess properties and owners should visit their assessor's office or check their web site for information about when assessments can be done, what period they cover, and how and when owner can appeal those decisions

- **Check the property description facts.**
  - **Dimensions and calculations.** Do this for both the house and the land to see that they are correct. If your lot or acreage is of an odd shape, be sure that is reflected correctly along with any easements that cut across your property.
  - **Damage or Defects in the property.** Make sure that the assessor has taken into consideration any defects in the property. Things like water damage to the walls, leaking roof or foundation, flooding after a hard rain, etc.
  - **Exemptions have been allowed.** Be sure that the assessor has credited you with any exemptions for which you may qualify (elderly, disabled, veterans, etc.).
  - **Type of construction used in the building.** A frame building will be valued differently than a brick one.

- Outbuildings and other improvements: Anything you have added to the home will add to the total value. Likewise, anything you have torn down and not replaced should be deleted from the value.
- The age of your property.
- Externally caused changes in property values. Look for things such as: zoning to a lower level, area flood damage (even though it may not be your own) including drainage problems, easements, heavy traffic, nearby railroad tracks, freeways, industry or toxic waste, etc.
- Property classification and usage. A single-family dwelling will be taxed differently than a multi-family dwelling.
- Depreciation allowance: Check both the computation of depreciation, and the appropriateness of the method used for calculating the depreciation. Examine depreciation factors, including the quality of materials, inefficient heating, structural cracks, deterioration, or chronic defects.
- Method of valuation. Find out what standard method of valuation is used by your district and determine if it has been applied appropriately.

- Compare your assessment to others. Property valuation requires a lot of opinion in making that judgment, as comparable properties and sales conditions can almost never be identical. If you purchased your property in the last two years and the real estate market has been relatively stable, the true market value of your property should not be much different than the price you paid for it . If you purchased your property more than two years ago, or if real estate values have fluctuated widely during your two years of ownership, you must begin to compile a list of other, similar properties in order to determine comparable value.
  - Comparability. Look at the assessment cards for all properties similar to yours to determine if there are any differences that stand out the can be used to build your case.

– **Market approach.** If your taxing authority's assessment method is based on market value (as is often the case), owners should ask themselves: Could I sell my house/unit for this much? If the answer is no, look at what comparable homes in your area have been selling for. You should conduct your comparison using at least three other similar properties. The more comparisons, however, the better your preparation of any appeal. Comparable means comparable in most ways: in the same school district, same number of bedrooms and bathrooms, same lot size. Use sites like Zillow.com and Cyberhomes.com to search sales data of individual homes/units. But keep in mind that you may not know the special circumstances that affect individual sales. If, for instance, a nearby house recently sold for a much lower price than what yours is valued at, it could be because it just had a flood in the basement. Also, some states, including Texas and Utah, are "nondisclosure states," which means their home sale prices are not matters of public record. If you're in a nondisclosure state, another option for finding sale prices is to ask a local realtor for sales information.

• **Make Your Claim.** Most appeals are submitted in written form to taxing units with a statement explaining why you think the valuation is inaccurate, how much you think your unit is worth and evidence to support that claim. In some places, there will be a hearing where you can present your case, after which you should be notified within a few weeks of the taxing unit's decision. Organizing your data for an effective and successful appeal will involve the actual preparation, timing and other logistics, strategy, documentation, approach, and knowledge of the idiosyncrasies, needs and preferences of your audience – the assessor and/or the members of the appeals board.

– Besides the differences between appeals based on errors in facts and those based on errors in judgment, there are several basic categories which most taxing units recognize for bases of appeals.

- *Unequal assessment* which results in an unfair property tax burden

- *Value that a taxpayer believes is too high* because the value was overestimated or appropriate exemptions have not been credited. Be sure you construct separate arguments for both of these items.

- *Improper property classification.*

– Your strategy should be customized to the type of appeal you are initiating. The following chart is an easy way to display the data and to present your case to the assessor.

Item in Contention	Error	Result
Estimate of cost to erect a building	By basing the estimate to erect the building on the manual issued by the state, the assessor arrived at a cost of $100,000. Actual cost of the building was actually $75,000, proven by the builder's contract.	Overvaluation of $20,000.
Cost of a back up emergency generator, wiring and other items connected to an air conditioning unit	These should have been classified as personal property. Manual lists exemptions for personal property.	Over assessment Of $5,000.
Estimate of square footage	Assessor's documents show 144 square feet of attached deck where it is actually 120 square feet.	Over assessment of $2,000.

Appendix T – Financial Management

Background:

Healthy finances are critical to the sound operation of a condo or homeowner association. There are many factors that come into play, including; accounting controls to protect the association's assets, well thought out and implemented budgets to ensure there is enough operating capital to over the ordinary expenses of the association, and detailed reserve studies to provide enough capital for future capital expenditures.

The Board of Directors is required each year to prepare a budget which estimates expenses for administration and operation of a condo or homeowner association during the year. It should include a reasonable allowance for contingencies and an appropriate contribution to a capital reserve fund for costs of future maintenance, repair, improvement and replacement of physical components. It is typically the responsibility of the Budget Committee, under the leadership of the Treasurer, to prepare an annual recommended budget to the BoD for approval.

The purposes served by the budget include:

- Sets the expense level for the association to carry out its functions and the assessment fee level to fund those activities
- Determines a plan for future needs and requirements and sets specific goals for future operations
- Forces the BoD and management to study the problems, needs, and quality of existing services and activities
- Helps the BoD or the managing agent to monitor performance of the association through the budget period to help identify adjustments that might be necessary

- Provides owners, lenders and management insight into the BoD's plan for the coming year and improves the board's ability to anticipate expenditures.

The budgeting process offers two opportunities for cost management. The first is budget cutting, which is essentially is reducing the current spending down to a specified level. The second is budget management which places more focus on preventing new or escalating costs from even entering the budget picture.

Budget cutting (reducing a certain amount/percentage from the entire budget or a specific line item) has become one of the most unpleasant tasks confronting an association's BoD. It seems as if "doing more with less" has become the norm for operating a condo or homeowner association. Since most associations have little in the way of unjustified spending to eliminate, there may be few easy targets. A BoD must approach budget cutting with care so as not to harm the association's capacity to achieve its mission.

Budget management can be a very effective method of controlling or reducing spending levels. With this approach, every cost is examined for reduction opportunity or elimination on a regular basis. It should be part of the mindset of the association and its leadership to continually ask themselves, "Is this cost necessary and is there any way to eliminate or reduce it?"   This is the ideal spot to control spiraling costs from occurring – at its source and before it is spent!

Data and Pertinent Information:

- An association's Treasurer is responsible for taking the lead on all budget matters and can include among other things the following roles and responsibilities:

- The Treasurer appoints other committee members (with Board approval) to the Budget Committee to assist in the execution of the responsibilities, as necessary.
- Consults with other association committees to review their last year's financial performance and determines their needs/wants for the upcoming budget year
- Reviews the financial statements (both the income statement as well as the balance sheet) to get a very clear picture of the association's financial position at that moment. This means including a review of the comparative budget for the current fiscal year.
- Reviews the most recent reserve study performed and determines if it is being properly funded.
- Develops and submits an annual budget and associated owner fees structure for the upcoming fiscal year to the BoD for approval.
- Monitors variances to the budget and submits reports at the BoD meetings.

- A budget segments the business into its components, or centers, where the responsible party initiates and controls action. Generally a single individual heads the responsibility center exercising substantial, if not complete, control over the activities of people or processes within the center, as well as the results of their activity. Cost centers are accountable only for expenses. The use of responsibility centers allows the BoD to pinpoint accountability. A budget also sets standards to indicate the level of activity expected from each responsible person or decision unit and the amount of resources that a responsible party should use in achieving that level of activity.
- A budget is a financial plan for future operation which has three major categories of expenses in a typical budget: Fixed, variable and capital replacement

- Fixed costs. Fixed costs those costs that do not vary with income and generally include items such as common area real estate taxes, insurance, maintenance contracts, labor cost, etc. These amounts are generally fixed annually.
- Variable costs can include such things as common area utilities, goods and services, snow removal, lawn care, staff/Management Company overtime, pest control, etc.
- Capital expense. The most common capital expense is a reserve category for capital replacement of major items such as the roof, parking lot repaving, replacement of clubhouse items, etc.

Conventional wisdom says that about 80 percent or more of your association expenses are fixed and you can't do anything about them. But, nothing could be farther from the truth. Every line on an association's budget should be considered variable and negotiable.

- Control reports are informational reports that tell the BoD about an association's activities. Accounting provides them with a format designed to detect variations that need investigating. Control reports need to provide an adequate amount of information so that a BoD may determine the reasons for any cost variances from the original budget. A good control report highlights significant information by focusing attention on those items in which actual performance significantly differs from the standard. Accounting control reports used to protect the association's assets include:
  - Balance Sheet
  - Income and Loss with variance
  - Detailed General Ledger
  - Cash Flow Report
  - Projected Payables
  - Delinquency Report

- – Check Register
- – Fully Reconciled Bank Statements
- There are several potential approaches do budget cutting.
  - – **Across-the-board cuts.** In some ways, across-the-board cuts are the easiest to administer. The primary analytical effort rests in determining the amount to cut. The association needs to determine the percentage of cuts that are necessary. When an association makes across-the-board cuts, the percentage is usually set and then BoD members/managers/committee chairpersons are asked to develop proposals for achieving the cuts in specific areas. This gives a BoD the flexibility to make the cuts where they will do the least damage to their operations. If budgets contain any slack areas, they quickly surface and will be the first to cut. The association may decide to consider multiple levels of reduction proposals, asking for budget reduction proposals at the levels of 10%, 20% and 30%. This process allows the BoD to evaluate the degree of cut that can be sustained in light of the disruption to programs and services.
  - – **Targeted cuts.** Targeted cuts can be identified and chosen by the BoD to achieve the required reduction. Targeted cuts may extend to higher impact decisions such as ending certain services, closing programs, or cutting back on support services. Such strong cost cutting moves will tend to bring larger reductions in costs but will come at a higher cost in member satisfaction.
  - – **Process or Technology-Driven Cuts.** One way to target cuts is to link them to process or technology changes. The association's staff or Management Company analyzes processes to identify ways to change procedures or apply technology that will reduce the work required. This strategy usually will not produce net savings in the short term and usually require time to implement.

- Another approach to finding budget cuts is to budget from the bottom up, which is commonly called zero-based budgeting. Many associations determine their assessment income and then allocate this income to various expenses. This is the inverse of what should be done. Instead, the budget should begin as a list of expenses. The disadvantage to using the income approach is that it leads to an unrealistic expectation of expenses. When gathering the expense data, use historical data, but also mix the historical data with expected service levels (e.g., snow removal) and anticipated changes in services and costs of services. Budget the expense categories with as much detail as possible. It is helpful to budget for expense categories as defined in the chart of accounts. For example, landscape maintenance may need to be budgeted as follows.
  - Landscape Maintenance:
    - Maintenance contract $X
    - Pruning $X
    - Fertilization $X
    - Landscape improvements $X

Recommendations/Alternatives to Be Considered:

- Create the right mindset. One of the most important things a BoD can do is to create the right cost-conscious mindset with all association members and particularly with the BoD and the Management Company, if one is used. BoD members should continually look for ways to reduce costs and to challenge every budget line item. Any cost increases should receive the highest level of scrutiny. Ask others to justify expenditures. Always, be on the lookout for ways to cut costs, even if they are small amounts.
- Your BoD should develop a written budget philosophy to help it decide what should be included in the budget and to also provide a stable and

consistent approach for managing the association's funds. Once established, you can now test it against all of your budget items to determine if there are any opportunities for cost savings. Shown below is an example association budget philosophy:

ABC Association
Budget Philosophy

The ABC Board of Directors has agreed upon the following budget philosophy to help it decide what should be included in the budget and to also provide a stable and consistent approach for managing the associations funds:

- Manage the association's money as if it were our own
- Only budget for those items that meet the following criteria:
  - Is this a non-discretionary expense to the association that
    - Is an obligation spelled out in the bylaws
    - Is necessary for the association to function
  - Is this a discretionary expense to the association that:
    - Is needed for the safety and security of the association or its property
    - Increases the overall value of the association property
    - Prevents a larger future expense to the association
    - Provides a desirable benefit to the overwhelming majority of members
- Target the reserve fund balance at a ____% fully-funded level for maintenance/replacement of long-term capital assets
- Whenever possible, offer optional participation for expenses that are discretionary in nature
- Obtain two to three competing bids whenever possible for contracted services
- Maintain a small contingency fund to respond to unforeseen conditions/opportunities
- Use Co-Owner expertise or volunteer labor to defray expenses whenever possible.
- Strategically use special assessments to cover the cost of non-reoccurring expenses rather than increasing association monthly dues.

Approved by ABC Board of Directors,_____

- Develop your budget from the perspective of zero-based budgeting. That is, for every expense line item in your budget, start with a budget of zero dollars and add budget amounts only as far as you can justify that cost. Be able to discuss the impact or expected results of the expenditures and what will be lost if the money is not spent. By looking to justify every line item, you may discover some items that are not necessary at all and others that do not need to be as large as they have been. This zero-based approach forces you to examine what you want to spend and make certain that the return is worth it. A BoD should set budget goals that challenge your BoD, Management Company, and association members.

- Establish and/or re-confirm the financial management reports that you will use to monitor performance. Some of these reports are designed to be used by the Treasurer to closely monitor detailed financial activities and others are designed to be used by the BoD and association members for summary information purposes. The Cash Flow Report is excellent high level 1-page summary report that summarizes the association's financial activity for the year.
  - Balance Sheet
  - Income and Loss with variance
  - Detailed General Ledger
  - Cash Flow Report (See *Appendix U*)
  - Projected Payables
  - Delinquency Report
  - Check Register
  - Fully Reconciled Bank Statements
- Now that you have developed a lean budget and have agreed upon your financial reports, you must closely monitor your on-going financial performance. Make sure that you review and use your accounting management reports. Quickly address any areas that need attention and develop contingency plans to bring any cost overruns under control. It is particularly important to do the following:
  - Examine all invoices before approval for payment
  - Review monthly or quarterly financial statements and budget performance
  - Review monthly or quarterly bank reconciliations
  - Monitoring the association's reserve funding and investment program

Appendix U – Sample Cash Flow Report

ABC Condo/HOA   20xx Cash Flow/Budget   10/31/xx

Font Key: bold font = actual, regular font = budget, italics font = actual + budget

	EOY	Jan	Feb	March	April	May	June	July	Aug	Sept	Oct	Nov	Dec	Total	Budget
Receipts															
Assessments	21600	21000	2400	24000	19800	1200	22800	20100	2100	21600	21000	2800	21600	180400	180000
Late charges & fees			240			190			210			220		860	880
Interest		12	12	1467	12	12	1575	12	12	1463	12	11	1228	5828	5000
Receipts Total		21012	2652	25467	19812	1402	24375	20112	2322	23063	21012	3031	22828	187088	185880
Disbursements															
Insurance				2827										2827	3000
Taxes				1287										1287	1300
Legal												400	400	800	4800
Electricity		424	212	230	254	268	272	284	289	296	259	300	300	3388	3500
Water		56		56		1847		4866		5218		3800		15843	16000
Irrigation maintenance					2170	1680	360	310	340	250	180	400		5690	6000
Grounds maintenance		1400	500	660	5300	11700	11780	4200	4400	4100	6450	4500	4500	59490	60000
Fence maintenance											13700			13700	14000
Snow removal		700	600	1700	600							400	800	4800	5000
Management		1400	1400	1400	1400	1400	1400	1400	1400	1400	1400	1400	1400	16800	16800
Administrative		135	127	524	137	155	1078	194	177	548	179	350	350	3954	4000
Mailings				233			247			241			250	971	1000
Meetings		1760			780			2230						4770	5000
Disbursements Total		5875	2839	8917	10641	17050	15137	13484	6606	12053	22168	11550	8000	134320	140400
Net Cash		15137	(187)	16550	9171	(15648)	9238	6628	(4284)	11010	(1156)	(8519)	14828	52768	45480
Cash															
Operating Fund Bal	3644	3769	3570	8653	17812	2152	3815	8431	4135	13682	12514	3984	5584	5584	1124
Reserve Income		15012	12	11467	12	12	7575	2012	12	1463	12	11	13228	50828	48000
Reserve Expenses								16800			19500			36300	40000
Reserve Fund Bal	146258	161270	161282	172749	172761	172773	180348	165560	165572	167035	147547	147558	160786	160786	154258
Petty Cash	250	250	250	250	250	250	250	250	250	250	250	250	250	250	250
Total Cash	150152	165289	165102	181652	190823	175175	184413	174241	169957	180967	160311	151792	166620	166620	155632

Appendix V – Financial Risk Management

Background:

Financial risk management is a structured approach to managing uncertainty related to a financial threat to a condo or homeowner association. Risk strategies include transferring the risk to another party, avoiding the risk, reducing the negative effect of the risk, and accepting some or all of the consequences of a particular risk.

Some traditional risk managements are focused on risks stemming from physical or legal causes (e.g. natural disasters or fires, accidents, death and lawsuits). However, in the context of condo or homeowner associations, financial risk management focuses on risks that can be managed using sound business financial practices.

Data and Pertinent Information:

A condo or homeowner risk management policies are part of a larger context shown by the following hierarchy:

Law

CCR's
& By-Laws

Financial Policies

Review & Audit Processes

Financial Reviews & BoD Reports

Typical Association Financial Structure

- The top level for the framework is Federal and State Law, including laws specific to Condo or Home Owners' Associations.
- The next level is the CC&Rs and bylaws that provide structure and rules for governing and managing the association.
- The next level Financial Policies comprise the collected policies and other key documents that govern the association financial affairs
- The next layer down is HOA financial Review and Audit processes. This includes both external audits and internal controls.
- The base of the hierarchy is the interface with association members through meetings, financial reviews and other communications. This is the financial affairs foundation that provides visibility and transparency for association members.

- An integrated approach for managing an association's risks will:
  - Enable the BoD, the Treasurer, Committee Chairpersons, and the Management Company Agent (if any) to work in a financially consistent manner.
  - Provide a framework and guidelines for making financial decisions by ensuring clarity about activities permitted, authorities; and accountability.
  - Define financial control and reporting requirements.

Recommendations/Alternatives to Be Considered:

- The following key governing components should be considered as a part of the condo or homeowner association's financial management risk plan.

ABC Association

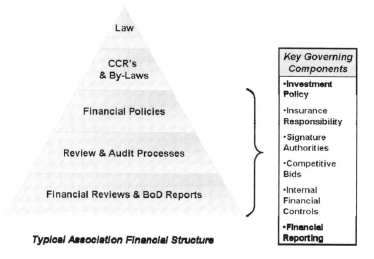

Law

CCR's & By-Laws

Financial Policies

Review & Audit Processes

Financial Reviews & BoD Reports

Typical Association Financial Structure

Key Governing Components
- **Investment Policy**
- Insurance Responsibility
- Signature Authorities
- Competitive Bids
- Internal Financial Controls
- **Financial Reporting**

- **Investment Policy.** To protect your reserve funds, every association needs to develop an investment policy that is formalized as a financial record of the association. This formalized investment policy is important as it provides a baseline and guideline for future BoD's, Treasurers, and Finance Committees. The investment policy should be structured around three elements, in order of importance; safety, liquidity, and yield. The majority of association invested funds result from the need to fund the replacement reserve schedule. A carefully planned and developed replacement reserve schedule will allow the association to match investments with scheduled reserve expenditures. Longer term investments will generally result in higher yields. Shown below is a typical association investment policy:

ABC Condominium Association
Investment Policy

The replacement reserves shall be invested in such amounts as may be authorized by the Board of Directors in accordance with the following policy:

A) No funds shall be deposited or invested except in authorized investments. Authorized investments are those that are in accordance with the declarations and bylaws of ABC condominium and that are obligations of, or fully guaranteed by, the U.S. government

B) All accounts, instruments, and other documentation of such investments shall be subject to the approval of, and may from time to time be amended by, the Board of Directors as appropriate, and they shall be reviewed at least annually.

C) Investments shall be guided by the following goals, listed in decreasing order of importance:

    1) *Safety of principal.* The long-term goal is safety of the replacement reserves.

    2) *Liquidity and accessibility.* Funds should be readily available for projected or unexpected expenditures.

    3) *Minimal costs.* Investment costs (redemption fees, commissions, and other transaction costs) should be minimized

    4) *Professional management.* Funds should be invested with professional manages who have good reputations and sound credentials.

    5) *Return.* Funds should be invested to seek the highest level of return that is consistent with preservation of the purchasing power of the principal and accumulated interest.

- **Insurance Responsibilities.** General risk management policy is to identify areas of risk, estimate the degree of risk, implement procedures and practices to reduce potential losses, evaluate which losses to retain and which losses to cover with insurance. Financial exposures for an association include theft of cash, fraud, embezzlement, loss of key records and business interruption, property and casualty risks, worker's compensation risk, and other liability risk in various forms. You should closely examine your insurance policies to make sure you are adequately insured. As a rule, all associations should have The association should be covered by a variety coverages which vary according to the property type and legal documents. Work with an insurance agent who has experience working with the specific needs of condo or homeowner's associations. The following examples are commonly used:

    – Property Damage, Hazard or Fire (Guaranteed Replacement Cost)

    – General Liability (common area injuries)

- Directors & Officers Liability (covers business judgments by the BoD)
- Workers compensation (protects against financial liability caused by injury to employees, Board members or volunteers)
- Fidelity Bond (protects against theft of association funds)
- Earthquake/Flood Insurance
- Employee Dishonesty
- Building Ordinance or Law (pays the increased reconstruction costs due to code and zoning changes)

While it is great to have insurance coverage to protect the association against a claim, it is also important to protect the association's insurance policy from repetitive or frivolous claims. Generally, when an association submits a number of claims to its insurer, it may either lose its coverage or the cost of the association's insurance policies will increase substantially. Therefore, we recommend that our community association clients engage in the following risk management techniques:

- **Risk avoidance.** An exposure is anything that can result in an insurance claim, like a slippery lobby or a cracked sidewalk. Part of the key to minimizing insurance costs is to reduce your exposures, to minimize them by doing what's called risk management or loss control. Most of them relate to common sense in providing the safest possible premises to avoid potential for bodily injury. Many steps can be taken to lower a building's liability with minimal cost including:
    - Ensuring that all doors are locked at all times, particularly out of the way basement doors and rear entries, lowers liability and increases the safety of the residents. Each

building also should practice good maintenance—no wet floors or trip/fall hazards

- If possible, you should update your building's electric, plumbing and central air conditioning. Update junction boxes from fuses to circuit breakers. Plumbing updates will reduce risks in some older buildings by lowering the probability of pipes bursting and causing expensive property damage. Make sure that your building's air conditioning drain lines and pans also are kept clean.

- Be sure that any contractor that is doing work on the property is properly insured. The contractor should have liability, worker's compensation, umbrella insurance and auto insurance. You also want an indemnification agreement.

- Installing sprinkler systems, burglar alarms and security cameras can positively affect a building's insurance rating

- Taking life safety measures for a building is always helpful in reducing insurance costs. One measure is to institute a fire safety program, in which the building's occupants are taught how to exit the building in the event of a fire.

- Insurance companies do an annual inspection of the property -- that's free advice. Those recommendations (of the insurance company) should be taken seriously

- **Risk control.** Risk control requires the association to maintain up-to-date records and to inspect the property periodically. These records will demonstrate that the association has not been negligent in its oversight of the property and in its maintenance duties.

- **Risk transfer.** Another important step the association can take to minimize the risk that claims are filed under its insurance policies is to transfer insurance risks from the association to the individual members. The association's insurance should typically be used for larger claims like wind, rain and fire damage that impact many units or other common area structures. Assuming the CC&Rs are silent on the issue, BoD's may adopt a policy that any loss attributable to an owner that results in a claim against the association's insurance, the owner shall pay the deductible. This is easy for owners to do if they have the deductible coverage that is an inexpensive addition to an owner's policy. Any such amendment should make it clear that owners pay the deductible when they are responsible for the loss, either because of their own negligence or because something under their control failed (such as a dishwasher, toilet valve, etc.) Tapping the owner's policy first is less costly for the association and makes the master policy do what it is supposed to do - insure the community against catastrophic losses.

- **Signature Authorities.** These delegate the BoD authority based on type and amount of expenditure. Signature authority policy requires that the signer(s) confirms that all appropriate approvals are completed. See sample below:

ABC Association Signature Authorities			
Transaction type	**Limit for Committee Chairperson or Management Company**	**Limit for Association Treasurer**	**Board of Directors**
Operating Supplies			
• Budgeted	$200	$1,200	No limit
• Non-budgeted	$0	$200	No limit
Capital Purchases			
• Budgeted	$500	$1,200	No limit

• Non-budgeted	$0	$0	No limit
Tax Returns and Tax Assessments	$0	No limit	No limit
Insurance Policy Renewal	$0	No limit	No limit
Legal Expenses	$0	$1,000	No Limit
Banking Services	$0	Association Treasurer is banking services administrator and establishes procedures per banking and investment policy	
Emergency Procurement	$200	$500	No limit
Invoice Approval	$200	$1,200	No limit
Credit Card	$0	$1,200	Only the President and Treasurer are authorized to use the association credit card
Petty Cash	$50	$100 The Treasurer will administer the petty cash fund	$250

- **Competitive Bid.** Large service contracts, such as Management Company, landscaping, pool maintenance, maintenance & repair, etc., should be competitively bid every couple of years. Other areas to which Boards should pay close attention to include: mortgage rates and lines of equity/credit; insurance coverage/premiums; fuel and utilities; laundry facilities providers; pest control; and elevator, boiler, and other mechanical component maintenance contracts. Guidelines should be established for competitive bids (sample shown below). Exceptions may be authorized for preferred suppliers who have been approved by the association BoD to be included on the "preferred supplier" list.

ABC Association Minimum Bids Required			
Amount of Procurement	Capital Expenditure	Goods and Materials, Operating Supplies	Contracts for Services
Up to $1,000	Not required	Not required	At discretion of Management Company or Committee Chairperson
$1,001 - $3,000	2 or more	At discretion of Mgm't Company or Committee Chairperson	2 or more
Over $3,000	3 or more	3 or more	3 or more

- Where applicable, written Invitation for bids should be issued that includes the item description and all contractual terms and conditions applicable to the procurement.
- Once a bid has been approved by the association BoD and the purchase ratified or the work begun, additional expenses incurred due to unforeseen circumstances or change orders should not exceed a specified amount of the original bid price (i.e. 10%) unless approved by BoD.

- **Internal Financial Controls.** The BoD is responsible for the financial well-being of an association including the proper safeguards and internal financial controls. A written internal financial control policy ensures constancy and continuity among current and future Board members. Internal controls are a system of policies and procedures that protect the assets of the association, creates reliable financial reporting, promotes compliance with laws and regulations and achieves effective and efficient operations. The following candidates should be considered for an internal financial control policy.

  - **Conduct an annual review.** An independent certified public accountant (CPA), selected by the association Board, shall conduct an annual analysis of the association's finances. The accountant shall have access to original books and records. In a review, the accountant investigates record-keeping practices and accounting policies and analyzes the statements. The accountant should prepare the disclosures on unusual items or trends that may require explanation. The accountant should also report any weaknesses in the association's financial systems, as well as issues concerning internal control, income tax, reserves, and document compliance.

- **Control reserve transactions.** The BoD must have full and separate control over the association's reserve account(s), including the signatory control of bank accounts. All transactions made by Board designees should be reported and verified in writing. These transactions should be approved by the BoD, and that approval should be documented in the BoD meeting minutes. The reserve cash funds should be separate from the operating cash accounts. A reserve study should be prepared every three to five years, and it should be reviewed annually. This study should be used in reviewing the adequacy of reserves as well as the funding and spending of reserve funds.

- **Adopt a BOD "Code of Ethics" policy** - The BoD should adhere to a written formal "Code of Ethics" policy to help maintain a culture of honesty and accountability with association members. See sample below:

ABC Association
Board of Director's Code of Ethics Policy

Truly ethical association BoD practices require more than a fear of legal consequences or a desire for a good reputation. Ethical business practices require a clear understanding of right and wrong, and a motivation on the part of directors, members and contractors to act in the proper manner at all times. This means adhering to not only the letter but also the spirit of all applicable laws and regulations. The following code of ethics had been adopted by the BoD to guide their activities:

1. The Board of Directors will use its best efforts at all times to make decisions that are consistent with high principles, and to protect and enhance the safety and property value of the members.
2. No gifts of any type will be accepted by any volunteer from any resident, contractor, or supplier that may be intended to unduly influence the judgment of the Board of Directors. Gifts of a nominal value and personal nature given as a token of friendship or on special occasions are acceptable. Likewise, entertainment that would be difficult to describe as "lavish" is acceptable. Cash gifts of any amount are not acceptable.
3. No contributions will be made to any political parties or political candidates by the association without a majority vote of the community confirming such action.
4. The Board Members will protect confidentiality of other Board Members' personal lives, as well as all association members' personal lives.
5. No promise of anything can be made to any subcontractor, supplier, or contractor during negotiations, unless approved by the Board as a whole.
6. Language at Board Meetings will be kept professional. Personal attacks against Co-owners and Board Members are prohibited and are not consistent with the best interest of the association. It is understood that differences of opinion will exist. They should be expressed in a clear and business-like fashion.
7. A Board Member may not knowingly misrepresent any facts to anyone involved in anything with the association that would benefit himself/herself in any way.
8. No Board Member may use his/her position into enhance his/her financial status through the use of certain contractors or suppliers. Any potential or actual conflict of

interest must be disclosed to the other Board of Directors.

9. No member may use any funds being held for condo association business for their own personal use. All finds must be segregated either through bank accounts or accounting records.

- **Maintain security of association documents.** Most financial records should be kept permanently because they chart the financial history and because they could contain information that would have a bearing on current decisions. This list includes the general ledgers and journals along with year-end financial statements, tax returns, audit reports and depreciation schedules. Financial records that might be subject to an IRS audit or to an accounting-related challenge include: accounts payable and accounts receivable ledgers, expense records, canceled checks, electronic payment records, purchase orders and vendor invoices. These records should be retained for at least seven years. Important financial documents, such as bank statements, deposit slips, budgets and petty cash vouchers should be held for at least four years.

  - Back-up records of essential information are to held at a secure location away from the property
  - The location of and account numbers for all bank accounts, including CDs and other savings accounts is held by BoD officers and included on the condo web site
  - A list of all vendors and copies of all contracts is held by BoD officers and included on the condo web site
  - A list of accountants, lawyers, insurance agents and others whom the community relies upon for professional guidance is held by all BoD officers and included on the condo web site

- Copies of insurance policies, including the name of the agent, and other pertinent information is held by all BoD officers and shown on the condo website

- Building plans, blueprints, "as-built" drawings, and contact information for the architects, engineers, contractors and sub-contractors who designed and built the structures are held by the BoD Secretary

- BoD decisions and meeting minutes, committee and business process documentation, and legal documents will be held by the Secretary and also contained on the condo web site.

- The condo website is backed up by the provider every day

- **Financial Reports.** The association Treasurer should reconcile bank statements or passbooks for all cash accounts and maintain a ledger that documents all financial transactions. Financial control reports are informational reports that tell the BoD about an association's activities. Control reports need to provide an adequate amount of information so that a BoD may determine the reasons for any cost variances from the original budget. A good control report highlights significant information by focusing attention on those items in which actual performance significantly differs from the standard. Any financial report should be accompanied by an explanation of any significant variances, such as significant cash surpluses, shortages, excessive accounts payables or receivables, or major budget overruns. Accounting control reports used to protect the association's assets include:

  – Balance Sheet
  – Profit and Loss with variance
  – Detailed General Ledger
  – Cash Flow Report
  – Projected Payables
  – Delinquency Report

- Check Register
- Fully Reconciled Bank Statements

Shown below is a typical schedule for financial reports.

Schedule of ABC Association Financial Reports			
Fund	*Statement Type*	*Frequency*	*Availability*
Operating Fund	• Income Statement • Balance Sheet • Cash Flow • Current Year Forecast Update	• Monthly • Monthly • Monthly • Quarterly	Recommended policy is that these be available to association members in multiple forms, including but not limited to the association website
Reserve Fund	• Current Balance • Current Year Forecast • Annual Long-Range Update	• Monthly • Quarterly • Annual	
Project Fund	• Cash Flow Summary • Invoice Tracking	• Monthly • Monthly	
Budgets • Operating Fund • Reserve Fund	– Income Statement – Balance Sheet – Non-Reserve Capital – Cash Flow – Year End	All Annual	

	Summary — Budget Year Detail — Annual Long-Range Update		
Special Reports	Financial Policy Update	Annual	Association website

ABOUT THE AUTHOR

Joe Kushuba is a retired executive from a large global marketing, engineering and manufacturing automotive company. His holds a master degree in Organizational Development and BS degree in Industrial Engineering. His educational and work experience background provides a unique blend of the soft sciences as well as the hard sciences that make him well suited for leading organizational change.

He has served as a Senior Advisor to several corporate CEO's, presidents and executive directors on matters surrounding large reorganizations efforts, global business strategy, organizational structure, decision support systems, business process reengineering, information management technology, and financial budgeting systems. He has extensive experience in team building, communication systems, conflict resolution, meeting management, and has led several large multi-national and global company mergers.

Most recently, Joe has brought this strong business background to the world of condo associations, where he currently serves as the President of his condo association since 2006. It was here that here he was able to develop and test many of the concepts described on this site and in the books that he has published.

Joe believes he adds value to organizations by helping them to become high performance teams, learn at accelerated rates, or to simplify their business.

INDEX

Administration, 15
approval group, 40
Arrear payment collection, 14
assessment and fee collection
    process, 107
association website, 127
beginning and ending date, 42
best alternative, 53
BoD "Champion.", 30
brainstorm for solutions, 51
budget, 19
Celebrating, 64
Certiorari, 18
collection policy, 94
Communicating results, 59
communications plan, 59
Complacency, 9
comprehensive implementation
    approach, 26
Controlling On-Going Costs, 11
cost creep, 9, 19, 57
cost reduction effort, 12
cost reduction initiative project, 26
decision package, 53
deep financial crisis, 26
deliverable, 26
diagnostic questions, 36
downloads, 13
electronic communication, 125
experience, 9
Financial exposures, 19
full sample project plan, 33, 47
ground rules, 32
Historic project data, 65
implementation process, 43
initial proposal, 30
Insurance, 16
Litigation, 17
major deliverable, 50
Management Company, 15

milestone, 42
nature of the project, 33
need for change, 10, 30
nemawashi, 47
No-Frills Approach, 21
on-going cost controls, 19, 57
perceived need, 35
possible causes of the problem,
    51
Preventative maintenance, 17
problem, 22, 36, 50
Project Champion, 40
project close-out, 63
project goal, 23, 38
project introduction, 33
Project Kickoff Meeting, 48
project management, 26
Project objectives, 38
project plan, 32
Purchased materials & services,
    16
quick-hitters, 14, 55
real estate tax, 18
Recognition, 61
Reserve funding, 17
risk management policy, 19
risk prevention, 20
scope, 34
shared vision, 29
SMART format, 38
tally sheet, 56
Taxes, 18
Team Leader, 41, 49, 57
Team Leader Instructions, 50
timing information, 42
Top 10 cost-saving return areas
    of opportunity, 14, 55
Treasurer, 30
tree structure, 26
Utilities, 15

Terms & Conditions of Use Agreement

RESTRICTIONS ON USE

This material is protected by copyright laws. You may not modify, copy, reproduce, republish, upload, post, transmit or distribute in any way any material from this disk without the express permission of Condo President, LLC., except for your personal, non-commercial use only. Readers and users agree not to sell copies of this document or otherwise seek compensation for its distribution.

LIMITATION OF LIABILITY

Under no circumstances, including, but not limited to, negligence, shall Condo President, LLC be liable to you for any damages of any kind (including, but not limited to, compensatory damages, lost profits, lost data or any form of special, incidental, indirect, consequential or punitive damages whether based on breach of contract or warranty, tort, product liability or otherwise) that result from the use of, or the inability to use, materials contained on this disk. This document is designed to provide accurate and authoritative information in regard to the subject matter covered. It is provided with the understanding that the publisher is not engaged in rendering legal, accounting or other professional services. If legal advice or expert assistance is required, the services of a competent professional should be sought.

9572664R0

Made in the USA
Lexington, KY
10 May 2011